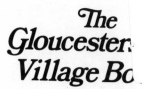

The
Gloucester
Village Bo

For Mr. Cee Bee

A small addition to
your valuable library from
which you so generously
lend.

Deram Digby

January 2019

THE VILLAGES OF BRITAIN SERIES

Other counties in this series include:

Avon*
Bedfordshire*
Berkshire*
Buckinghamshire*
Cambridgeshire*
Cheshire*
Devon*
Dorset
Essex*
Hampshire*
Herefordshire*
Hertfordshire*
Kent
Lancashire*
Leicestershire
& Rutland*
Lincolnshire*

Middlesex*
Norfolk*
Northamptonshire*
Nottinghamshire*
Oxfordshire*
Powys Montgomery*
Shropshire*
Somerset*
Staffordshire*
Suffolk
Surrey
East Sussex
West Sussex
Warwickshire*
West Midlands*
Wiltshire
Worcestershire*

*Published in conjunction with County Federations of
Women's Institutes

The Gloucestershire Village Book

Compiled by the Gloucestershire
Federation of Women's Institutes from notes
and illustrations sent by Institutes in the County

Published jointly by
Countryside Books, Newbury
and the GFWI, Gloucester

First Published 1987
Reprinted 1990
© Gloucestershire Federation of Women's Institutes 1987

Countryside Books
3 Catherine Road
Newbury, Berkshire

ISBN 0 905392 87 6

Cover Photograph is of Minchinhampton
by June Turner

Produced through MRM Associates Ltd, Reading
Typeset by Acorn Bookwork, Salisbury
Printed in England by J. W. Arrowsmith Ltd., Bristol

Foreword

The Wolds, the Forest, the Vale: a brief but accurate description of Gloucestershire, this most beautiful of English shires, and one which contains the basis of its history.

Great historical events took place in our county. Gloucestershire was the heart of Roman England. The Forest of Dean and the river Severn provided a bulwark against the 'recalcitrant' Welsh. Edward II was murdered in Berkeley Castle. By virtue of its central position, Gloucester became the seat of Parliament for the travelling Kings of England and subsequently supported the Roundheads in the Civil War. But it is not only royalty which has shaped the destiny of Gloucestershire. There was agriculture, sheep and the woollen industry which brought riches and a number of crafts which survive to this day.

You will find these facts mentioned in this book along with many other more local memories of Gloucestershire villages, and you will perhaps understand the hours of patient and willing research undertaken by many W.I. members and friends to make this an indispensable guide to our county.

We are grateful to all who have contributed and we express regret to those whose contributions had to be edited or omitted through lack of space. We know that all the contributors have derived a sense of achievement and enjoyment from their task, and we hope all who read the result will share our pleasure in this book.

Sybil Everitt
County Chairman

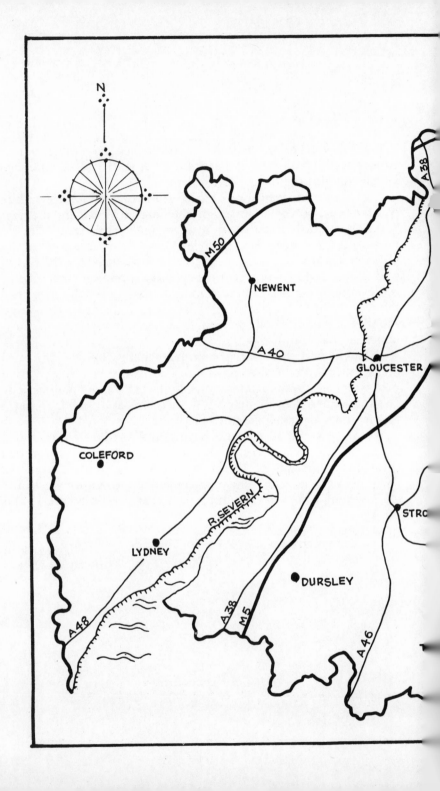

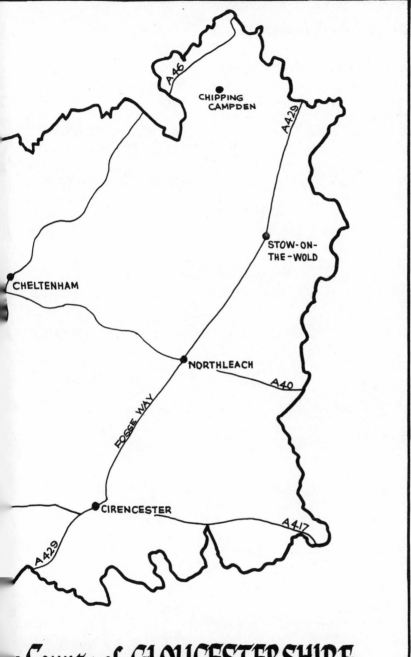

CHIPPING
CAMPDEN

A46

A429

STOW-ON-
THE-WOLD

CHELTENHAM

NORTHLEACH

A40

FOSSE WAY

CIRENCESTER

A417

A429

County of GLOUCESTERSHIRE

Acknowledgements

The GFWI wish to thank all the Institutes whose members worked so hard to provide information about their villages and to Margaret Sollars, Andrew Kennett and Dr. A. Excell who provided additional information for the book.

Our thanks to Peggy Ward, Mona Frow and Martha Matthewman for their excellent line drawings, and to Molly Timbrell for the line map of the county.

Finally, a special thank you to Ann Kennett, the co-ordinator of the project.

Ampney Crucis,
St Mary & St Peter 🪶

The roots of the Ampneys go back at least to Saxon times. We
have an Iron Age fort just beyond our boundary, and there are
important Roman remains in Barnsley Park. Both the Church of
the Holy Rood at Ampney Crucis and that of St Peter in the village
of that name have definite Saxon features. That of St Mary may
have pre-Conquest remains.

Secular buildings do not go back so far in history but Ampney
Park, the 'big house' of the area, still stands in its extensive
grounds to the west of the Church. This was owned by the
Pleydells in 1561 according to the records. Their original gabled
Cotswold Manor House had additions in the 18th and 19th
centuries. Its crowning glory is the main room which has a
Jacobean ceiling with pendant bosses, panelled walls and a carved
stone fire-place and overmantel bearing the Pleydell arms and the
date 1625. Many of the village cottages date from the 17th century
or earlier. Until late in this century new building work was kind to
the village but latterly some of the infilling has not been so in
keeping with the rest.

While the Ampneys cannot compete for tourist attraction with
the real 'honey-pot' villages of the Cotswolds, all have corners that
the discerning appreciate. In Ampney Crucis it is the first section of
the lane that straggles up through the village from the A417 near
the Crown of Crucis that delights all comers at all times of the
year. To the east the stream meanders down behind the Crown,
past an old mill and some cottages, before being bridged by the
A417. To the west are old cottages with lovely gardens going
down to the brook. Over the bridge is a small green with a replica
of the old cross at its centre. A side lane, overhung with trees,
passes more cottages on the right with the churchyard on the left.
It ends just beyond the church at the entrance to the old stable yard
of Ampney Park. The churchyard contains one of our principal
treasures. This is the exceptionally well preserved 15th century
cross. Its gabled head was found walled up inside the entrance to
the rood loft, by the 19th century restorers. It had been immured,
possibly to save it from destruction during either the Reformation
or the Civil War.

Although there are traces of wall paintings in the church of the Holy Rood it is to Ampney St Mary one must go to see paintings in profusion. This church, now isolated in fields on the bank of the brook, lies about a mile further to the east along the A417. It is very small, and used to be covered with ivy, thence its pet name, the Ivy Church. As well as the wall paintings which probably date from the 12th to the 15th centuries it has a rare survival in the shape of a stone screen. Even now it cannot be used in the winter as there is no heating and it is lit only by candles. It is, even so, very popular for special ceremonies such as christenings. No one knows why the village disappeared around the church but it is the one-time hamlet of Ashbrook that is now known as Ampney St Mary. This is at least ½ mile due north of the church.

St Peter's Church contains what is possibly the oldest relic of them all. In fact it may be pre-Christian. It is the carving of what is considered to be a fertility symbol. The village itself ranks as an area of the greatest charm. Although now hardly more than a hamlet, it is very compact. Each cottage looks every inch a Cotswold Cottage and all are in complete harmony with each other and the surroundings.

Andoversford 🥀

Whoever comes to Andoversford is always on his way to somewhere else, or so it seems. Even the busy little river Coln which rises a few miles to the north of the village has a great future elsewhere, for it is off down the gentle eastward slope of the Cotswolds to join the Churn, the Windrush, the Evenlode and all the other little streams which eventually form the Thames and 'go to London to see the Queen'.

Way back in prehistoric times, the ancient trackway, now called the 'Jurassic Way', which crossed the country from the Bristol Channel to the Humber, forded the river Coln here, then the Windrush at Naunton, before continuing north-eastward through Stow-on-the-Wold. How many of those long-ago travellers stopped here to camp beside the sweet, clean water of the little Coln before continuing on their journey?

Nowadays Andoversford lies in a cat's cradle of new roads to Gloucester, Cheltenham, Stow and Oxford with the busy A40 trunk road forming part of the pattern. The rumble of traffic is never far away but most of it passes by, leaving the village, once the scene of so much activity to get by as best it can.

On the outskirts of the village is the Frog Mill, a rambling, much enlarged wayside inn, known to have been a corn mill in Norman times when the marshy ground beside the river was probably alive with frogs. Early in the 18th century it had become a coaching inn – the first on the road between Cheltenham and Oxford. Passengers were brought up by chaise from Cheltenham to board the coach here and much has been made of the rivalry between the landlords of the Frog Mill and the Andoversford Inn down in the village for they were on different routes to Oxford in those days and it appears that neither was above taking down or altering the direction posts in order to catch the passing traveller!

The Andoversford Inn still stands, square and dignified, down in the village, but nowadays it is well off the beaten track while the Frog Mill, ever expanding, displays its bars and restaurants and gardens out along the main road with the Coln, alder-fringed hurrying by where the mill wheel once turned.

In the 19th century new travellers appeared and Andoversford found itself with a railway station when the line from Cheltenham to Cirencester was opened, but both this and the little branch line from Andoversford to Stow are now closed. The station is a builder's yard, the old railway line a pleasant green footway through the hills. The old hump-backed road bridge over it is still there, marooned among the fields while the new Gloucester road swoops by beside it.

Arlingham

'If I had to leave Arlingham I'd leave this country altogether' vows John Bircher, farmer and parish councillor of this old village, deep in the great horse-shoe bend of the river Severn south of Gloucester. In fact, he would go further and happily build defences across the mile-wide open end of the loop, thus making Arlingham into an island defended against all comers! It has to be said that this rejection of the outside world has probably been aggravated by recent tangles with Local Authorities, both lay and Church, seated in Gloucester, which have decreed the closure of the village school.

11

This school, once bursting with children, now stands empty and up for sale. Gleefully, John says: 'The Church Commissioners can't sell it. They want too much for it!'

But Arlingham was not always so far away from the world as it seems today. A mile away from the centre of the village, down the old drovers' road, in the middle of the loop, is the ancient river-crossing to Newnham on the west bank. From here the Romans began their penetration into the Forest of Dean by crossing the sands and currents at low tide, some believe with elephants, as elephant bones have been dredged up on the Newnham side! Much later the Saxons came to grief on these same sands as they tried to follow the fleeing Britons across the river.

Here, too, the Welsh drovers, bringing their cattle down through the Forest of Dean to be sold in London, would drive them down to cross the river at low tide. The herds would have to swim from the Newnham side but those who knew the river well could guide them the rest of the way over the sand bars to the pastures around the Old Passage Inn at Arlingham. From there they would follow the wide, straight road, with deep drainage ditches on either side, through the village and on towards London.

It is said that it was possible to ride, or even drive a carriage across the river here, but woe betide any stranger who tried it, for the Severn here is notoriously dangerous and it was best to trust the ferry man who knew what he was about.

Now, the whitewashed Old Passage Inn looks out across the water towards the red triangle of Newnham cliff topped by its little church spire, a tumble of trees and houses down its shallow eastern slope. The ferry no longer plies between Newnham and Arlingham Passage but the inn is a favourite spot with summer visitors who can sit outside on the rustic benches and watch the changing face of the river, now dawdling along on the Newnham side, with great stretches of gleaming sand and shallow pools between, alive with calling water birds, now a powerful upstream flow as the Severn Bore goes by, reversing the direction so that if you stay there long enough, you will see, perhaps, a branch that floated by you in the morning come hurrying back again in the afternoon. In winter, the water echoes with the cries of the wildfowl which come here to feed on the rising tide – wild swans and geese, winter visitors from Greenland and Scandinavia calling and gabbling or rising with a great clatter of wings to wheel away towards the Wildfowl Trust's reserve a few miles down river at Slimbridge.

The 14th century Arlingham Church, its squat tower crowned with a pretty traceried parapet, stands on slightly rising ground on the edge of the village looking out over the flat surrounding pastures to the river on three sides. In the north wall of the nave you can see the gorgeous colours of some of the oldest stained glass windows in the county. Six hundred years have gone by since stone mason Nicholas Wyshongre was paid seventeen shillings and a bag of wheat for each foot of the tower that he completed and the church has seen many a disastrous flood in the years between. Opposite the church is the gateway in mellow time-worn brick to the now vanished Arlingham Court, a beautiful tudor mansion which, late in the 19th century, simply collapsed, neglected and overgrown with ivy, and has now been demolished. Ivy is everywhere, crawling along the churchyard wall of huge old stones and rosy, time-worn brick, and adorning the fronts of cottages, though the steep gables of Church Farm are now clear of it, whereas in old photographs it wore a thick coat through which the windows peeped.

These days, Arlingham doesn't grow, as many Gloucestershire

villages do, though cottages tumbling down with age are renovated and often, if they are beyond repair, they are completely
rebuilt. But by and large it remains a place of dairy farms and
orchards, peaceful and remote in the crook of the Severn's arm,
although not so far away the M5, the A38 and the railway all pass
by en route between Gloucester and Bristol.

Ashchurch

Ashchurch is very different from the normal village, being a
collection of several hamlets. These are Fiddington, Aston-on-
Carrant, Pamington, Aston Cross, Ashchurch itself comprising the
church, school and a small cluster of houses with the Village Hall
and War Memorial as the centre, Natton and Northway. Until
quite recent times Northway was just fields with a scattering of
houses and farms but now is a very large housing estate which
seems to be ever-growing. The whole parish area is now much
more prosperous than formerly when agriculture and the railway
were the only large employers. But now that most of the population goes to work in the surrounding towns it means that the
villages are in danger of becoming merely dormitories and not
communities in the real sense of the word.

There used to be a Quaker church at Natton. Ashchurch House
itself has been demolished and the ground used for the new
Tewkesbury School. Northway House was an hotel from 1949
and has recently been remodelled as a pub. The new Northway
shops now stand on the site of what was once a lovely rose garden.
The other big house in the area is now a home for disabled people
and it is interesting to recall that this house, named Walton House,
was once the property of the parents of the novelist Barbara
Cartland. The Village Hall was built in the 1920s and replaced an
earlier wood building which was burned down. There is a small
Methodist Chapel standing on the outskirts of the village which
has been in use for almost a century but is now, alas, to be used no
more. A new Methodist Church uses the Community Centre at
Northway. This area now has two churches and only the Parish
Church of St Nicholas can truly be said to be in the centre of the
village.

The station at Ashchurch was demolished by British Rail in the

14

1960s when they closed down the branch lines and the station ceased to be used. It was a charming little place being stone built in an attractive style and the waiting rooms were always polished and welcoming with flowers and magazines, while the platform flower beds were always colourful in the summertime. How ironic that, after pressure from local people, the station will be reopened again (if money difficulties can be resolved).

Many of the black and white cottages in the area have gone but fortunately there are still a number in all the hamlets, saved by the revival of interest in old buildings, but the blacksmith's shop in Pamington is no more as are the shops which were once a feature of Aston Cross until quite recent times. Gone too are the farms and fields where the Army Camp now stands. This was built in 1938/9 and it covers up a footpath which ran directly from the old Methodist Chapel to the Parish Church.

The cricket field at Pamington still flourishes, although balls are prone to get lost in the adjoining Thirle brook which flows through the parish and the new copse which was planted in Pamington recently. This land and the cricket field have been donated by a local farmer who takes an interest in the environment.

One old custom that older residents remember is being given a loaf of bread if they attended church on Christmas morning, and there was coal for the elderly. In more recent times this charity has been diverted to the giving of a home-made biscuit to each member of the congregation after the Midnight service on Christmas Eve.

Ashleworth 🍂

When Robert Batsford sold his cottage at Ashleworth Quay in 1961, he bequeathed his waders and elver nets to the new owners. He would not, he said, be using them in Cheltenham! And who would have thought, on a sweet May morning, seeing the Severn sliding smoothly between ten foot banks, green meadows adrift with buttercups, the church spire gleaming among the chestnut trees, that waders would ever be needed at Ashleworth Quay? But often, in those days, when the winter snow melted in the Welsh mountains, the Severnside farmlands would be inundated and Quay dwellers needed waders to escape from cottages marooned by the floods.

Ashleworth, however, like other riverside villages between Gloucester and Tewkesbury is built mainly on the western scarp, half a mile from the river, out of reach of such floods, but, strangely, the little steepled church, massive 125 foot tithe barn, and once fortified manor house (now known as Ashleworth Court) are close to the water. The lane from the village passes them and then comes to a full stop at the Quay where the Boat Inn and a few cottages look out across the river.

Here, until the turn of the century, there was a chain ferry across the Severn to Sandhurst. Horse-drawn barges travelling up from Gloucester had to follow the east bank as far as Ashleworth to avoid the marshy land on the west side, but here, the horses were ferried across to continue their journey up river to Tewkesbury and beyond along the towpath on the Ashleworth side. Needless to say, while the horses were rested and fed in the stables, which still stand beside the road, the bargemen were similarly entertained at the Boat Inn. The ferry was kept busy carrying vehicles, goods and passengers to and fro while, in spring, local farmers used the little jetty for sheep dipping, the creatures being dumped off the end into the water and having to swim round to the shore!

For many years after the chain ferry's demise, Ted Jelf of the Boat ran a punt service across the river and kept the old pub virtually unchanged. They say that when the mains water was laid on a few years back, Ted, by then stiff with rheumatics and unable to get down to the kitchen, was never told by his daughters of this innovation. He would never have countenanced such dramatic changes!

The famous Severn Bore which attracts great crowds along the estuary below Gloucester swishes past Ashleworth in two distinct waves as the river has been divided lower down by Alney Island and one side has travelled further than the other.

With the Spring tides come the elvers. Experienced locals can judge by the state of the river, and the weather, when they will come, but come they do, and with them the elver fishermen with their great spoon-shaped nets and their all night fires along the banks. Several times lately a silly young seal has been seen chasing up river after the elvers, a long way from home in the open sea!

Old Ashleworth, grouped prettily round its village green and straggling away along twisting flowery lanes has seen rapid change in the last few years. Though the charming hotch-potch of old houses remains, there is also a good deal of new building and with the new houses come new people.

Relatively new, too, are the Duckeries, a lovely stretch of unspoilt wetland beside the river between Ashleworth Quay and Hasfield. Leased by the Gloucestershire Trust for Nature Conservancy from a private land-owner in 1968, it is now the winter refuge of thousands of wildfowl – shelduck, mallard and teal; divers such as pochard and goldeneye, native waders like snipe and curlew and, now and then, a graceful family of Bewick Swans. The reserve sports a well camouflaged roadside hide, hardly necessary in times of flood when the steely water's edge creeps close to the road bringing fleets of ducks almost within arm's reach, bobbing on the ripples with their heads facing into the wind.

Nearby stands the enchantingly beautiful half-timbered Ashleworth Manor, built in the 15th century for Abbot Newland of the Abbey of St Augustine at Bristol. Tradition has it that the house was a summer residence for the Abbot and later, after the Dissolution of the Monasteries, it became the property of the Bishops of Gloucester. This lovely house, with its heavily carved ceiling timbers and many other interesting features, is now a comfortable family home but is open to view by written appointment.

Avening ☙

As one approaches Avening from the Tetbury side, the first view is one to enchant the eye. In a little hollow the Cotswold village lies serene and peaceful, with Gatcombe Park, home of H.R.H. Princess Anne and Captain Mark Phillips in the distance.

Avening has had its troubles as most villages have, but these troubles happened 900 years ago with a first-class scandal. It began and ended with Royalty, and not many villages can boast of that!

What is now Avening Court was at the very hub of it. Brittric, a young Saxon nobleman who lived at the Court was sent on a mission to Baldwin, Count of Flanders, and there he met Matilda, who later became the wife of William the Conqueror. The story goes that she fell in love with the handsome Brittric, but he refused her, and this so infuriated Matilda that when in later years she became the Queen of England she remembered this slight and trumped up a charge against him and he was thrown into Worcester Prison where he languished for years and eventually died. On hearing of his death Matilda, in remorse, ordered the building of Avening Church so that prayers could be said for the repose of his soul.

The Church was dedicated on Holy Cross Day, September 14th 1080, and it is thought that the Queen gave a feast on this day for the builders. Now in alternate years the people of Avening re-enact the Feast with parishioners taking the roles of Queen Matilda, the Abbess of Caen, Nuns, Archbishop Lanfranc and other dignitaries, and the Feast is preceded by Festival Evensong in the Church that Matilda built. For many years the Sunday nearest to September 14th was called Pig's Face Sunday and the numerous pubs in the village served Pig's Face Sandwiches containing a brawn made from pigs' faces to all customers. This custom has now been discontinued.

In the late 19th century Avening bell-ringers wanted to increase their peal of five bells to six and decided to steal one from the nearby village of Cherington. The plot was carried out but after hanging the stolen bell the men discovered that they had taken the wrong one and when they were found out they were charged and imprisoned for several months. In his summing-up the judge said that, had it not been that the theft did not benefit the thieves personally, the penalty would have been death.

The village used to boast at least seven public houses but these are now reduced to just one, the Cross Inn. The main meeting-place for the village is the Memorial Hall, a strongly-built hall, built by public subscription in memory of the large number of the men of the village who gave their lives in the First World War and a handsome extension has recently been added to improve the facilities available.

There were three mills in the village, all powered by the stream which runs through the centre of the village. One of these is still standing and is used for light industry and offices, and the foundations of the other two may still be seen.

Three ancient cottages in Woodstock Lane were once the village Workhouse.

The pinnacled Fountain at the Cross was erected by parishioners to the memory of William Fowles, a member of a family once prominent in village affairs.

In the grounds of the Old Quarries can be seen the entrance to an ancient prehistoric burial chamber, removed from a hilltop near Nag's Head for safe keeping.

Many interesting people have lived in Avening and they include Mr H. Dickenson who was a pioneer in X-ray technology and was also the owner of the first motor car seen in the village.

On his retirement Lord Lee of Fareham came to live at Old Quarries (now the Home Farm Trust) and while there he had a gallery built to house some of the pictures from the National Gallery, dispersed for protection during the Second World War. His banner, formerly hanging over his stall in St George's Chapel, Windsor now hangs in Avening Church.

Aylburton 🦢

The 14th century Preaching Cross stands centrally in the village to the west of the main trunk road A48. To avoid accidents the Cross was moved from the centre of the road to the side. High Street extends for a quarter of a mile with shops, post office and cottages on either side, affording no chance for road widening. Half a mile to the west, at Lower Common, 16 houses are built on the rock, locally known as 'Honeymoon Row', so-called because the houses were first occupied by newly weds!

St Mary's Church is unique in that in 1856 it was decided to bring the church nearer to the people, and it was moved stone by stone from Chapel Hill and erected on its present site in the same Early English style of the 13th and 14th century. Each August the distribution of the Willoughby Charity takes place and has done since 1681. The story goes that Christopher Willoughby, who lived in Wiltshire, was travelling through the village and had trouble with the wheel of his coach as night was falling. Asking for help, he was refused by two families, but the third helped and gave hospitality. The record says his wife was born in the village. In his will he left £16 to be distributed annually to poor people born in Aylburton, except descendants of the families who refused aid.

There was no Non-conformist church in the village before 1915 when the present Methodist Church was built. The first services were conducted from the steps of the Cross, and from 1912–1915 services were held in the old Malt House.

The typical village school was built in 1869 of grey Forest stone and consisted of three classrooms and a school house. The scholars took two or three pence per week to pay for their education. The behaviour of children in those early days seemed to cause much anxiety – climbing on roofs, breaking tiles and pipes. The churchyard opposite was a great attraction, particularly at nightfall, and this no doubt accounted for the 'ghosts' that wandered around at dusk!

The religious and social life of the village has been much helped by the late Viscount Bledisloe who lived to a great age. In 1920 he gave the site for the Memorial Hall, and the playing field in 1936. His wonderful influence greatly helped the character of the village, and whatever undertaking was started the villagers made it a success. Lord Bledisloe's mother founded the Aylburton Cottage Hospital in 1882, and in 1908 it was moved to its present site in Lydney.

The village was very active during the Second World War, many working at the Bacon Factory (which was visited by Queen Mary), NAAFI, assembling gas masks, nursing, caring for many evacuees including, at the Mansion, Princess Juliana and her family from the Netherlands, and the famous Girls School, North Foreland Lodge, evacuated from the perilous position on the north-east coast of Kent.

Today we are fortunate in having a Thermo Insulation factory in the village, as well as several factories nearby, Lydney Park Estate and several farms. We have several fishermen, and in season, can enjoy freshly caught shrimps and salmon.

With co-operative effort and good neighbourliness the community spirit exerts itself to the full in the village.

Beckford 🐝

The village stands on the site of a Roman-British settlement. Archaeological finds on Bredon Hill include a Roman kiln and pottery. Coins bearing the superscriptions of several Roman Emperors have also been unearthed.

The church's Norman nave was constructed in the 12th century.

On the column by the pulpit are some unusual Norman carvings. The windows form a comprehensive series of five different styles of architecture over 300 years.

Beckford Hall has an extensively chronicled history of conflict between the various incumbents and successive monarchs over their religious laws. It became a Priory in the early 12th century and in 1247 Beckford church was let to the Prior. It became the Manor during Henry VIII's suppression of the 'alien priories'. Peace came in 1586 when it was bought by Richard Wakeman, a prominent Roman Catholic, and remained in his family until 1836.

In 1884 the Ashton-Case family settled at Beckford Hall and the Captain built two wings, one of which contained a lovely chapel where the Catholic villagers worshipped until 1974. From 1936, until the Hall was sold to a building developer, it was the House of Novitiate of the Salesian Fathers of Saint John Bosco. Nearby is Court House, behind the west end of the church where sheep stealers were tried and, in some cases, hanged for their crimes in the Dalton House/Old Vicarage grounds.

Many people will have wondered why Beckford village looks different from the other Bredon Hill villages. Where are the black and white thatched cottages? They were there once, the Beckford Inn to the right of the church, the cottages next door and opposite, Dalton House on the left, all bordering the village green and market place, with a path across the middle. Suddenly they were gone, devastated by fire. Even the brick-built Old House was extensively damaged although Dalton House survived.

The railway opened in 1866 bringing a new kind of life. The New Inn was built in 1774 and became a very busy place and an important landmark. Once a fortnight there was a cattle market in the field opposite, where now three houses stand. Cows, pigs, sheep everything converged on Beckford by road and rail. The New Inn was re-named the Beckford Inn and the landlord was even allowed an all-day extension. Sadly, the 'Beeching axe' dropped on the Cheltenham to Evesham line in 1964. Only the Station House, platforms and bridges are still in place, but the Beckford Inn still looks much as it must have done to travellers from the railway carriages.

By the 1930s there were several shops along the main road; a cobbler, Rocklands Stores, a garage, a butcher, a post office and

21

even a small chapel. Fifty years on there is still a blacksmith but all the rest have gone. The same thing has happened in the middle of the village; two bakeries, a coal merchant, another post office, the village school; all have been closed. However, the village shop with post office has survived, there is another garage on a different site and a successful silk printing business has been developed in the old vicarage.

Berkeley 🦃

Berkeley is dominated by its ancient castle which was built in the time of Henry II for the Earl Robert Fitzharding. Henry also had a lady love nearby in Frampton, fair Rosalind. The castle has a shell keep and the building is now a noted tourist attraction. It was lived in as a family home without tourists until the late 1950s. The Berkeley family still live in the castle. One of the great sights of the castle is the huge breach in the western wall which was blown there by Cromwell's guns during the Civil War. Cromwell gave the castle back to its owners with the proviso that the hole should never be filled up again, which it never has been.

No mention of the castle can leave out the infamous toad. He was reputed to be of gigantic size and to have leapt forth from the centre of a great stone when the quarrying work for the castle was taking place at Stone. So evil and venomous was he that no one knew what to do with him so they put him in the dungeon of the keep and he fed on the hapless prisoners thrown in there. Even in recent times Berkeley mothers frightened naughty children with tales of the toad!

Very near to the castle stands the ancient and beautiful parish church. There is a table tomb immediately on the left of the door. It is of a former mayor of the town and its rhyme is very special:

> Here lyeth Thomas Pierce whom no man taught,
> Yet he in iron, brass and silver wrought.
> He clocks and jacks and watches with art made,
> And mended too when others art did fade,
> Of Berkeley five times Mayor this artist was,
> And yet this mayor this artist was but grass,
> When his own watch was down on the last day,

He that made watches had not made a key,
To wind it up so useless it must lie,
Until he rise again no more to die.

On a modern kneeler you will also see Berkeley's famous Witch. Her legend is too long to include here but if you go outside to the back of the church you will see her on a pinnacle being carried off by the Devil which was her ghastly fate. The Berkeleys' Mausoleum opens off the chancel and although it is generally locked you will be able to look in through the glass window at the splendid tombs.

Berkeley's most famous son was born here in 1749. He was the surgeon Edward Jenner. He was apprenticed to a surgeon in Sodbury and studied under Hunter the great anatomist. Jenner was practising in Berkeley when he decided to put a piece of folklore to the test. The story went that milkmaids who got cowpox didn't get smallpox. Jenner infected a boy called James Phipps with cowpox taken from Sarah Nelmes and a Red Gloucester cow. A month later he infected him with active smallpox. Nothing untoward happened – and the rest is history. Very recently Jenner's house has become a museum largely due to the generosity of a Japanese millionaire Mr Sasakawa. Edward Jenner was buried here, where his father was vicar.

Berry Hill 🐑

'Look, Mum, pink sheep!' Many a carload of children have been enchanted by the appearance on the roadside of such apparitions as these, for, along the roads around Berry Hill, the sheep are the residents and you are the visitor. Red, pink, blue, green, turquoise, we've seen them all, for, although the freemen of the Forest of Dean regard the grazing of their sheep as an absolute right, it is necessary to use these coloured markers in order to claim your own. Strangely enough, the sheep don't mix much. You rarely see a medley of colours for the old ewes keep to their own part of the forest and teach their lambs to do the same. A pity they don't teach them some road sense too, for, although the experienced matriarchs can graze nonchalantly along the verges, one provocative leg out on the road, without a glance at the passing traffic, there's never a spring goes by without a few casualties among the lambs.

Berry Hill, like many forest villages is an untidy mixture of old and new buildings drifting along the meeting of roads between Coleford and Ross-on-Wye, Monmouth and Mitcheldean. The Forestry Commission has, in recent years made great efforts to open up the Dean to visitors and a fine caravan and camping site has been opened nearby, named Christchurch after the church at Berry Hill.

At Edge End on the other side of the village there is a way-marked forest trail through towering beech woods, interspersed with more recently planted conifers, a delight in spring when the beeches put on their brilliant green, or in autumn when they are glorious in rust and gold.

Beside the main road to Monmouth is the Royal Forest of Dean School for the older children from a large surrounding area. Fleets of buses carry them to and from the school – which is modern with a huge assembly hall and everything up to date. But what lucky children to have the forest on their doorstep – though no doubt many of them would gladly swap it all for the lights of the city!

Beverstone ఇ౿

Beverstone is situated not very far from the main A46 road, on the road from Calcot to Tetbury. It has a church, ancient barns and a lovely little ruined castle.

The castle is a real gem but it is easily passed by without being noticed as it is hidden by farm buildings. It has had a chequered career. In 1051 Earl Godwin, Harold and Harold's brother stayed here whilst their army, camped on Uley Bury, terrified poor Edward the Confessor. In 1145 the hapless King Stephen held it against a siege by his own mother Queen Maud. In 1360 it was completely rebuilt and refurnished with ransom money from French prisoners taken at the Battle of Poitiers. In the Civil War it was captured by the army of Parliament whilst its constable, Colonel Oglethorpe, was out courting a girl at a local farm. Since then it has collapsed into a discreet ruin. It still has very sound Norman piers and the lower part of the tower still stands. Inside it still has a lovely little early English hall with a side chapel equipped with a 'squint' window so that its lord could be feasting in the hall whilst still attending mass through the window. The castle is still opened very occasionally for charity and should not be missed on one of these occasions, as it is a gem of its kind.

The church is very near the castle as one would expect. It was rebuilt six hundred years ago by Thomas, Lord Berkeley. The castle itself was an early seat of part of his family. Its tower has a Norman base and the doorway too is Norman with beautiful foliage decoration. The pulpit is a stone one, ornamented with leaves and flowers. There is a beautiful oak chancel screen with a little story all its own. It was obviously disliked by some Victorian incumbent who had it removed to his garden to act as a rose trellis. However it was saved in time and is back where it belongs no worse for its ordeal. On the wall of the church is a charming little 18th century carving of Sarah Shipway with long curly hair.

Near the castle is one of the village's two remaining large barns. The most famous of the village barns, Calcot Barn, came to an unseemly end. The barn was built in 1300 by Henry, Abbot of Kingswood to gather in his great tythe. However, in what amounts to medieval 'jerry building' Henry had the great beams made of Spanish chestnut instead of English oak. Late in the last century they gave out and the barn fell down. It was never rebuilt and the roofing stone disappeared across the sea to Ohio where it was used for the roof of a church at Marie Mount.

Bibury
with Ablington & Winson 🌿

These three villages lying close together along the river Coln, are separate yet inexorably held together by bonds of proximity, common heritage and ancient tradition. Although the district attracted settlements as far back as the Iron Age it was the Saxons who caused the emphasis to shift from the wolds to the river valley. The Saxons were farmers who cultivated the wolds, but their settlements (the beginnings of the present villages) were in the valleys. They needed waterpower for grinding their corn and chose the sites for their mills so well that these have remained unchanged for centuries. This applies to Bibury's Arlington Mill and Winson

Mill (both of which were mentioned in the Domesday Book) and to Ablington Mill.

The church and chapels of Bibury, bestowed on Osney Abbey in the 12th century, became exempt from diocesan jurisdiction, with strange repercussions later. In the 13th century the villagers of Bisley failed to cover a deep well there, causing their parson to fall in and drown. In the 15th century, during a brawl in Bisley churchyard, blood was shed on consecrated ground. These events caused the authorities to forbid all burials within the Diocese. Bibury, however, being outside this jurisdiction, agreed to set aside part of its churchyard for the burial of Bisley parishioners. This ground in Bibury churchyard is known to this day as 'The Bisley Piece'.

The mills and the churches provided the focal point round which the villages developed. The local stone was used to build the walls and roofs of the cottages and farms, and many of these, hundreds of years old, still survive. Examples are Ablington's massive tithebarns and Bibury's Arlington Mill. In the Middle Ages the whole district prospered with the growth of the woollen industry, and the wealth of the wool merchants created a legacy of large houses and memorials. In later times, however, sheep farming fell in importance with the general decline in the woollen industry, but in recent years the district has found a new prosperity in its natural beauty, tourism and improved transport.

For a spectacular view go to the top of Ladyhill or wander up from the mill to Arlington where ancient stone houses nestle close together, all higgledy-piggledy as if they were houses just put down at random. The names of cottages: The Old Bakery, Weaver's Cottage, Spinner's Cottage and Mill Cottages indicate activities no longer carried on. Or go up the hill towards Aldsworth and see the delightful circular dovecote in a lane on the left, known as Packhorse Lane or The Saltway. It was once the track along which salt, that precious and essential commodity for preserving meat during winter, was transported by packhorse. Almost opposite is the Coln St Aldwyn road which gives a breathtaking view of the magnificent Jacobean mansion Bibury Court, lying in a bend of the river and backed by wooded hills.

From Bibury Trout Farm the road rises sharply to Ablington. Old cottages and farmhouses with delightful gardens lie on the slopes down to the Coln, and further along past the old Mill

Cottage the river banks are covered with daffodils in the spring. No longer does the mill grind corn or generate electricity to 'The Big House', nor does the brewery provide refreshment as it did in times gone by. Ablington does not even possess a shop or a garage. But you may see a team of horses being driven four-in-hand, or a hot-air balloon rising majestically from a hidden field.

From Ablington you go over the bridge towards Winson, along a tree-lined lane used by walkers, horseriders, hunters and cars. The church stands at the highest point of the village, a simple structure with neither tower nor spire, but with several unusual and ancient features. On the shafts of the porch can be seen several votive crosses crudely carved and initialled or dated. These were probably inscribed by parishioners about to embark on a long journey or pilgrimage as a pledge that they would make a gift to the church if they were spared to return. The village of Winson lies mostly along the loop road that starts at the church, and many professional and retired people live here. The houses are old, and stone-carving is much in evidence, as on the gateposts of Old Manor Farm and Winson Mill Farm.

Bisley

When the picturesque Bisley Wells were restored in 1863 by the Rev. Thomas Keble (brother of the founder of Keble College, Oxford), the tradition of the Blessing of the Wells began.

Every Ascension Day since then, with the exception of a break in the war years, the tradition has continued. It is a great event in the village calendar which maintains the feeling of excitement which must have been felt in the past when holidays and entertainments were so much rarer than they are today.

The first preparations start with fund-raising efforts — coffee mornings, bingo sessions or even a disco — to raise money for the children's teas and to pay the brass band.

Then moss and flowers have to be collected to cover the frames and hoops carried in the procession by the older children. I have heard that in the past, when children stayed at the village school until 14, they used to decorate them at home in secret and there was great rivalry, but these days the frames and hoops are decorated in school with the help of teachers, mothers and even grandmothers, some of whom took part in the procession as children themselves.

There is a yearly anxiety whether there will be enough flowers. Ascension Day always seems to fall before or just after the first flush of May flowers and everyone scours their garden for blooms and even resorts to begging neighbours and friends for anything that is out, as large quantities of flowers are needed to cover the large stars carried by the oldest children. Somehow, however, the task is always accomplished and the finished garlands are left in the cool air ready for the morrow.

On the afternoon of Ascension Day there is a short service in the Parish Church. Then the procession forms in the school playground. It is in strict order of age with the four oldest children having the privilege of carrying the large stars at the front. Preceded by the brass band and the vicar, the whole procession winds its way along the High Street to the Wells where the vicar stands in front of the Wells and a further brief service is held.

The children then arrange their flowers to spell the word ASCENSION and the year, concluding with the youngest infants placing their posies around the Wells. After a final hymn and

28

prayer the crowd disperses; the children to their tea provided by a committee of helpers.

This is followed by village sports in the evening with traditional races such as the sack race, the three-legged race and the egg and spoon race with prizes for all the winners.

It is a truly village occasion when one feels the continuity of village life, knowing that the children are enjoying things experienced by their parents and grandparents and even if the ceremony only dates back as far as 1863 the spirit of the day seems much older.

Blakeney 🎋

Blakeney with Awre and its surrounding hamlets nestles in a valley between Lydney and Newnham-on-Severn on the A48 Gloucester to Chepstow Road. Small cottages dot the surrounding hilly countryside (known as Little Switzerland) together with dairy and beef farms. Blakeney stands at the confluence of two biggish streams, one of which runs under the house and shop of the village Post Office. The Post Office house dates back to the 18th century and was originally a small police station with a 'holding cell'. In fact the cell bars are still to be seen in the owner's office.

There are roughly 1,500 inhabitants many of whom work in the local industries, light haulage, woodworks, fruit farms and some travelling by coach daily to Cheltenham and Gloucester to larger industrial concerns.

Salmon fishing is still carried on in Gatcombe (one of the small hamlets) and at Poulton Court Farm – a moated Tudor manor house. Net making is also continued at Court House, Gatcombe. There is also a house called Drake's House at Gatcombe where it is believed Sir Francis Drake stayed while visiting the Forest of Dean to buy timber for boat building.

The Forest of Dean was one of the oldest and most important of the country's iron-making centres and this industry existed at numerous places around Blakeney. There were a number of forges around, possibly one at Furnace Bottom in the village. Cinders were brought from English Bicknor for use together with a one-third charge of iron ore. The resulting pig iron was taken up Pig Street thence to Gatcombe and on to Bristol via the old Severn

Railway Bridge. This of course has disappeared, only leaving us with the names.

Beer and cider brewing also existed early in the 20th century but all that remains of those industries are the cider presses that are still dotted around the area. In fact there is one in very good working condition at Gatcombe.

There has been an influx of new people to Blakeney over the last ten years and together the new and the old have combined to keep alive the village atmosphere.

Awre remains what it has always been, an agricultural community, although it has declined in importance in comparison with Blakeney. Latterly too, it has shown a tendency to become a dormitory for people working elsewhere and a good place for retirement with its place of solitude in a curling arm of the Severn.

But what of Blakeney? With most light industry being directed to Lydney and Cinderford it rather looks as though attention should be turned to tourism. Beginnings have been made towards this end with the establishment of the Dean Heritage Museum at Soudley, so perhaps the future augurs well for Blakeney.

Blockley 🌿

In Dovedale Woods is the source of Blockley Brook, the very life-blood of this ancient and prosperous community, nourished by water pouring out from the permeable Oolitic Limestone that forms a cap over the Cotswolds. The Brook never dries up in the severest drought and has for more than a thousand years provided the power to turn the water-wheels and led Michael Drayton, the Warwickshire poet, to refer in his *Poly-olbion* (1613) to 'that most springfull place where out of Blockley's banks so many fountains flow!' Twelve mills are recorded in Domesday Book, all engaged at first in grinding corn but many later converted into silk mills when, for about two hundred years, silk-throwsting made Blockley one of the most populous villages in the North Cotswolds.

Going northwards from Dovedale is a dammed-up artificial lake providing a waterfall of some height. Here Lord Edward Spencer-Churchill inserted a water-wheel, which ran a dynamo, making electric light with which the Northwick family's Dovedale House was lit. This was in the early 1880s, making Blockley one of the first villages in the world to have electric light. A year or two later the Astral works at the other end of the village lit the church, the streets and many of the houses as well as the village store, owned by J. Joyner.

Still going northwards along the High Street Fish Cottage is on the left. During the first half of the last century here, in a pool in the garden, lived a tame trout which made Blockley famous throughout the world. It was fed and tamed by William Keyte and when it was brutally murdered by some jealous or drunken neighbour in 1855, William Keyte's son put up an oak Memorial board to their pet fish:

IN

MEMORY

OF THE

OLD FISH

UNDER THE SOIL

THE OLD FISH DO LIE

20 YEARS HE LIVED

AND THEN DID DIE

HE WAS SO TAME

YOU UNDERSTAND

HE WOULD COME AND

EAT OUT OF OUR HAND

DIED April the 20th 1855

Aged 20 YEARS

Rock Cottage was the secret retreat of Joanna Southcott, the prophetess, from 1804 until her death in 1814. At that time Rock Cottage was leased by the Bishop of Worcester to John Smith of Blockley to whom she was secretly married in 1814. John Smith and his friend George Troup, Equerry to the Prince Regent, are buried close together in the churchyard. A devout Southcottian, Miss Alice Seymour, belonging to a distinguished family and herself related to Lord Fortescue, bought Rock Cottage in 1917 and turned it into a Centre of the Southcottian Sect. Publications poured out from Blockley and Southcottians came to visit this shrine from all parts of the world.

After a disastrous fire at Rock Cottage in 1971, the items from

Miss Seymour's extensive Southcottian collection which survived the fire were acquired by Blockley Antiquarian Society and with later valuable contributions from Southcottians in New Zealand now form one of the finest collections in the world of manuscripts and printed works concerning that Millennarian Sect.

A house now called Widdowe's Close was formerly a grocery, and it was here that Elisha Smith Robinson invented paper bags for shoppers. These were manufactured by the Robinson firm of Bristol.

Blockley's first mention in history is in a charter dated AD 855 in which Burgred, King of the Mercians sold the so-called 'monasterium of Bloccanleeh' (with little relation to the modern meaning of 'monastery') to the Bishop of Worcester to help finance his war against the Danes.

Blockley, originally in Worcestershire now in Gloucestershire, was the second biggest place in the former county at the time of Domesday Book. The population reached as much as 2,600 inhabitants when the silk trade was at its most prosperous. After that trade was killed by French competition none of the attempts to replace it by other small factories succeeded, the village suffered from great poverty and the population sank to just over 1,800, at which it has remained apart from the temporary influx of about 1,000 Poles during the Second World War. The success of a new small industrial estate and some other possible developments now point the way to a rosier future.

Bourton-on-the-Water 🎐

Bourton is mentioned in the Domesday Book after the Norman conquest, as being the property of Evesham Abbey. A stone-built church, probably about 1100, replaced an earlier wooden Saxon one. Since then the church has been rebuilt three times and registers go back to 1654. It is thought that a tunnel runs from the 14th century chancel to the Manor House opposite, where a dovecote dated 1400 still stands. During the Civil War Bourton Rectory gave shelter to Charles I and his son on their way from Oxford.

Most of the old houses in Bourton were built in the 16th and

17th centuries from local stone. The oldest pub is the Old New Inn which has a sundial marked 1712.

Bourton was a humble agricultural village and it has not lost sight of its farming origins. It had, within living memory, a cattle market, three corn mills served the village and the river Windrush was diverted from its natural course to drive them.

The bridges for which 'The Venice of the Cotswolds' has become famous were built between the 17th and 20th centuries.

A woollen industry developed in Bourton, but had died out by the 17th century.

Many old inhabitants remember it as a self-sufficient village with its mill, its forge, its saddlers, its slaughter-houses, its butchers and bakers and its pharmacy. There were outfitters for ladies and gentlemen, and shops that sold everything from a pin to a suite of furniture. The old bearded carter, Mr Bishop, went round the Cotswolds delivering grain; George Oakey drove sheep from Little Rissington to his slaughterhouse and butcher's shop in Bourton, and in the 1920s Mr Butt was taking some of the first photographs.

Charter-fairs were held in the main street on the first Fridays in May and June – and are still held. Years ago every child in the village was given a penny to spend at them by the Lady of the Manor. With such a lovely river flowing through the village what boy could resist playing football in its clear waters – and they do so still!

The Moore family lived in Chardwar, built in the 16th century as a farmhouse – they were great benefactors of the village, leaving their name to Moore Road and the Moore Cottage Hospital. This hospital began as a hospice in Fox's Yard, one of the oldest houses in Bourton. Today the village is very proud of its hospital on its new site in Moore Road.

The railway came to Bourton in the late 1800s, bringing perhaps the first visitors to the village, but with the closing of branch lines it has gone for ever. But the new era was undoubtedly heralded in by Jack Lake who made village history by driving Bourton's first motor-car for the doctor.

Since then thousands of people have come by car, no doubt first of all to see the Model Village. This was built by 'Bo' Morris of the Old New Inn in his garden and he was persuaded to open it to the public. Thousands of youngsters have seen the little houses with delight, and thousands too have been to 'Birdland', opened by Len Hill in the 1960s in the grounds of Chardwar house, to see the macaws, the tropical birds, the penguins, the tropical flowers and plants.

Today Bourton has approximately 3,500 inhabitants and a Parish Council that works hard to ensure the well-being of those who live there. Care is taken to keep the greens immaculate, the river clean and the inevitable litter problem under control. Together with the Conservation Society they scrutinise planning applications and the village is vociferous at the Annual Parish Meeting.

We are still a thriving village community and the person who wrote 'The village has an unreal delicacy about it – some corners look more like a film-set than real life', doesn't know what we get up to when the visitors have gone!

Boxwell with Leighterton ꙮ

These two delightful Cotswold villages are very near each other; Boxwell to the west and Leighterton to the east of the main A46 road from Cheltenham to Bath.

Leighterton is a tiny but lovely village with an ancient church whose tower dates back to the time of King John. It has a fine oak timbered belfry and spire. The church's finest possession is its lovely 14th century font which is richly decorated with carvings of representations of the Passion. They are a seamless vest, a hammer and scourges, four nails, a cross, a ladder, a spear, a sponge and a crown of thorns. One panel of the font is left plain – no one knows why. In the village cemetery are the war graves of Australian airmen killed during the Second World War when they were stationed at Leighterton Airfield.

Very near to Leighteron lies the hamlet of Boxwell. It seems strange that such a tiny place has so much history but indeed it does!

Ancient Boxwell would appear to have had a nunnery which was sacked by the Danes. Nothing remains of this establishment but the great well known as 'The Boxwell'. True to its name the well rises in the midst of a huge stand of box trees believed to be one of the biggest in England. The well is marked on the map as

'St. Mary's Well' and it was considered to be efficacious in the healing of weak and inflamed eyes. This use was continued until early in this century by local people. The well rises in a great pool which feeds a pond in the garden of Boxwell Court.

The church is a fine one with a high nave and a 700 year old font. It has a lovely little bellcote similar to that of Harescombe near Gloucester.

The great manor house, Boxwell Court, has a fine claim to fame. It was here that Charles II hid as he fled from the ruinous defeat of the Battle of Worcester. In the house they still hold relics of his visit: the bed he slept in and a ring he gratefully gave the lady of the house.

Bream 🌿

Someone once said of Bream that it 'looked as if it had been dropped from a great height', and certainly if you stand at the top of the village beside the 'Rising Sun' and look out over the random scattering of miscellaneous buildings you would feel inclined to agree.

However, Bream has its roots deep, deep in the secret past of the Forest of Dean, when iron was mined long before the Romans penetrated this far and improved the technique of digging and smelting the ore. (There's many a forester even today who will vow that we probably taught them rather than the reverse!)

The village began as a clearing in the vast royal forest where King John hunted for deer and wild boar, passing this insignificant settlement by, to stay at the great castle of St Briavels not far away. For centuries the foresters have clung to their ancient rights to graze their animals, and later, mine the coal in the Dean, and many a tale is told of the running battles between hard-pressed employees of the Crown and the locals, who, bit by bit, extended the boundaries around their cottages, poached the deer and stole the timber, all of which they maintained was theirs by right. At one point in 1831, a party of Redcoats was sent down from London to try and bring some order to the scene, and a local ringleader, Warren James, took refuge in one of the many old mine shafts nearby until he was finally betrayed, tried and deported, never to be heard of again.

But it was the Industrial Revolution which brought the sudden explosion of building to this forest village. Coal mines appeared on all sides, and houses, shops, bakeries, shoemakers, inns and more inns, sprang up without a thought to planning, and the whole place was humming with life. Now the storm has passed, the village is blown apart, the mines are left as a fascination to the industrial archaeologist, and old men sit with their memories of the mining days, the lamp-lit processions home from work through the dark, the courting down the Parkend Road before the street lighting came, the cinema with its twopenny seats, the fights and brawls with the lads from nearby Whitecroft and Pillowell.

The 'Princess Royal', last of the mines, was closed in 1962 and with the closure came the end of an era.

The 17th century 'Rising Sun' has seen it all! It still looks out over the rugby field towards the far ridges of the forest (now mainly of conifer trees planted by the Forestry Commission) broken here and there by a few green clearings and a scattered village or two. The rugby players used to meet at the 'Rising Sun' but now they have a smart new club house down the road. There is a sports club too, and the village boasts more than one brass band and a male voice choir.

Not far down the road at Pillowell lives Malcolm Bassett whose fame as a dog trainer has spread far and wide. You have never seen such rapport between man and dog as you watch his little working collie climb ladders, balance on see-saws, run through tunnels, twist to and fro between stakes and finally leap on to a pedestal, and all for the love of the game! Malcolm's Forest of Dean team which included his daughter Lisa, then only thirteen, and her little collie bitch won the Agility Class at Crufts in 1984.

Many new people have come to live in Bream. New houses stand cheek by jowl with old, renovations go apace, and there is even a new group of Westbury Homes named the Maypole Estate. How many future children will be able to show you where, until it was cut down in 1926, the village maypole stood on a small patch of green where two roads meet at the edge of the village?

Brimscombe & Thrupp

The villages of Brimscombe and Thrupp together form the parish of Thrupp. The name Thrupp means both a hill or steep spot, or equally a collection of houses or people, and both are apt to describe this parish.

It is an area of contrasts. There are beautiful old Cotswold houses, which give the impression that time has stood still since the spacious days of sheep and the wool trade. Beside them are the humbler dwellings of the one-time mill workers. From the valley road the hill rises steeply to an area known as the Heavens.

Down in the valley lie the mills, not obtrusively Satanic, but somehow characteristic of the Cotswold scene. The making of West of England cloth has vanished from this area, but now, there is a range of products being made, a tribute to local enterprise and adaptability of local workers.

Griffin Mill founded by the Griffin family in 1600 turned from the making of cloth to the making of furniture. Ham or Home Mill is now spinning carpet yarn for the Bond Worth organisation.

When the Thames and Severn Canal was cut in the late 18th century, a Brimscombe site was chosen for the headquarters building in front of which was a large sheet of water known as Brimscombe Basin, and on the far side of this stood Port Mills, now after years of making cloth, occupied by Benson's International System.

The most famous building is Lypiatt Manor, now the home of Prince and Princess Michael of Kent. It is reputed to be haunted by the ghost of a blacksmith who made the beautiful iron gates that front the manor. Judge Coxe, who owned the house at the beginning of the 18th century had sentenced the smith to death for murder, but reprieved him until the work was done.

Strangely, there is no church in the parish and residents are obliged to travel to worship. There is a primary school and until the Second World War, there was a secondary school. That is now closed, and older children travel to Manor School at Eastcombe.

Some years ago great efforts were made to provide the parish with a focal point for social activities. This Brimscombe and Thrupp Social Centre is serving its purpose very successfully. Brimscombe and Thrupp are good places to live and work.

Brockworth 🖋

Broco-wardinge is mentioned in the Domesday Book; 'wardinge' meaning homestead by 'broco' – brook, this being the Horseferry (now Horsbere) Brook, which flows from Witcombe, through the village alongside the old Norman church with its now familiar square tower, dedicated to St George in 1142. A pre-Roman settlement was sited here and many antiquities and coins have been found. Adjacent to the church and its graveyard (which has become full up in 1986!), is Brockworth Court Farm, the old Manor, built in fine Tudor style in the 1530s, one of the oldest buildings in the village; it stands along an old 'Salt Way' from Droitwich to the South Cotswolds, now re-named Court Road, although its original name still exists the other side of Ermin Street, namely Green Street. Many notable families have lived at the Court – De Lasne, Chandos, Guise, Priday and Morgan. Sir Christopher Guise had a marble bust of himself placed in the church during his lifetime so that he could go and look at it from time to time!

That prominent landmark, Coopers Hill, lies to the south of Ermin Street and is 820 feet above sea level. Here, too, there was an Iron Age fort and to the east are the ruins of a Roman villa near Coopers Hill Farm which generates much interest. Roman snails are still found around its slopes! The Whitsuntide 'Cheese Rolling' ceremony dates back to pagan times with connections in worshipping the sun, though the association with the sowing season, fertility rites and the scaring of evil spirits seems justified. The ceremony continues under a committee of local people who believe it preserves the rights of the common. With television coverage this old custom has become known world-wide. In 1970 the common was bought by Gloucestershire County Council and it is now a nature reserve through which the Cotswold Way winds.

In 1900 Brockworth was a straggling village of some 1,760 acres, with a population under 500. The character of the village altered radically when Gloucester Aircraft Company was formed in 1915. New housing estates were built on Westfield, Ermin Park and Court Road areas for the increasing population, followed in the 1950s by those on Moorfield, Pound Farm and more recently,

Abbotswood. Today there are almost three thousand homes and the population is nearing 10,000!

Gloucester Aircraft made many famous aircraft including the Gannet, Gloster Gladiator (the last bi-plane) and during the Second World War the Hurricane and Typhoon. The first ever jet fighter, the Meteor, took to the skies in 1952 followed by the Javelin Delta Wing. Today the old aircraft hangars form part of Hucclecote Trading Estate.

In 1939 Timberlands, Brockworth and Witcombe Hostels were built for war workers. Abbotswood estate now stands here today. Brockworth even boasted of a cinema in the war years! Armstrong Siddeley took over part of the factory to make jet engines followed by Hawkesleys who manufactured pre-fabricated houses – one complete house was made very 18 minutes! Some of them still stand in Ermin Park today yet they were only supposed to last 20 years! British Nylon Spinners took over in 1961 becoming part of ICI Fibres in 1964 and countless miles of nylon have since been manufactured.

Due to new motorways, traffic problems in Ermin Street have greatly increased and it is hoped that soon the bypass will be constructed to help alleviate the continuous traffic flow through the centre of the village.

Bussage & Brownshill 🎋

The two settlements of Bussage and Brownshill – for they can scarcely be called villages in the true sense of the word – cling to the hillsides above the Golden Valley of Chalford, within whose civil parish they lie.

In medieval times the whole of the area formed part of Bisley common, some rough grazing and some open fields, belonging to the Manor of Bisley. The Cotswold breed of sheep provided the wool for the cottage industry of weaving, and the stone was quarried for houses. As the textile industry grew, so did the population and settlers enclosed tiny parcels of land, built their cottages and occupied them, gradually pushing back the borders of the common. By the 18th century many of the sites now occupied by houses in Brownshill, and around the minute village green at Bussage were already enclosed, and the present pattern of roads – then only donkey tracks – was established.

Many people found employment in the mills of the Golden Valley – St Mary's, Dark Mills and Wimberley Mills amongst others.

Until the 19th century the spiritual needs of both places were overseen by Bisley Church (probably in a very perfunctory way!). However, in 1839 a group of Oxford undergraduates, inspired by J. H. Newman, subscribed to build a church at Bussage. The first site chosen was nearer to Brownshill than now, but the local builder rejected this on geological grounds as Fullers Earth led to frequent slipping of the slope. Instead the church was built below the existing cottages, by Bussage Hill, and increased the scattered nature of the place.

An intense and sometimes loud dispute took place between the very strict Anglicans, with their Tractarian traditions, and the Baptists who had a chapel at Eastcombe. A drunken minister at the latter led to a secession of members, who set up a meeting in a room at Bussage House, specially built by the squire William Davis and equipped with a new organ from his own works. The Meeting room lay just across the road from the church and many summer evenings would resound with organ music, swelling to over-shadow the austere chants of the Anglicans. Most times the 'Dissenters' won!

The Baptists eventually returned to their Chapel and the room became a school for boys, run by John Sibree, whose name is perpetuated by a road on the new estate. One pupil described it as being like Dotheboys Hall – a total contrast to the National School established by the Parish Church which went from strength to strength. Another Victorian building on the edge of Bussage, it had a site which gave little chance for expansion, but was replaced by an ultra-modern school in the new part of the village in 1983.

What of Brownshill? It never received its own Anglican Church, but a 'House of Mercy' was established in 1851 at Brownshill House to rescue 'prostitutes and fallen women', run by the vicar of St Michael and All Angels, Bussage. It continued under the original Mother Superior, Grace Poole, until 1898, but closed soon after the turn of the century. Following a chequered history, the house, lying off Blackness Hill, is now home to a Roman Catholic congregation.

The visitor, walking around either Bussage or Brownshill, will be struck by the number of small, old cottages. This pattern stems from the 19th century, which was not a generous one to the inhabitants. The woollen industry was depressed and factories had not become established as a means of employment. Few people had the means to improve their living conditions, and the few large houses date from before 1850 – the two already mentioned, Skaiteshill House, built in Classical style, and the old vicarage, now called Old Glebe House. Their owners were not of old titled families, but rather 'local men made good' by farming, quarrying or trade.

Cam ෯

This ancient parish is growing at a tremendous pace experiencing much bigger growth even than that during the period of the Napoleonic Wars and after, when the cloth mills boomed in the valley, even importing workers from Yorkshire and Lancashire to work the machinery. At that time the parish was split into two separate ecclesiastical parishes: Upper Cam, St George's, the original church and Lower Cam, St Bartholomew's, with a new Victorian church. The present boom in housing started in two stages in the early 1950s and early 1970s. It has converted much of the old parishes into a gigantic housing development.

This has meant many changes for the locality and unfortunately some losses have been made.

The river Cam dominates the lower part of the valley and has in fact gouged out the whole of the great valley in the past. It rises above Uley and meanders its way towards the Severn. Its name comes from the Saxon word for crooked and it is named in the same way as its more famous cousin in Cambridgeshire.

All the free water in the valley is still technically owned by the woollen company who have the first rights to its use. Once the village had a unique 'Boiling Well' with bubbling water. The water was not hot but filtered through a naturally porous stone which made the water bubble. Regrettably it has recently been destroyed by vandals.

The Victorians built a lovely little railway 'The Dursley Donkey' which ran through the valley to the main line at Coaley. It suffered Dr Beeching's axe and died like so many others.

The oldest church in the village, St George's, has several notable features. It has long been believed in Cam that William Tyndale

42

was born here and christened in the Norman font. The church's choir stalls are built in Tyndale's memory and bear his coat of arms. The church contains some pleasant features like the ancient font and lovely Jacobean pulpit and altar table (which you can only see well on Good Friday). Outside on the tower you will notice the animals present in local mumming plays, the Dragon, Horse, Ox and Green Man. At the east end is the church's most celebrated memorial, a table tomb with the figure of a man ploughing inscribed in the stone. The chains of the plough are flying through the air towards the man's head. It is believed that this is the tomb of a man struck down for ploughing on a Sunday but there is no documentary evidence.

High above the village are the two 'Slip-Outliers' – hills which have fallen off the main Cotswold massif. They are called Cam Longdown and Cam Peak; both have the look of volcanoes, which they are not. The smallest hill, Cam Peak, has the rare distinction of having been built by the Devil. Legend has it that 'Old Nick' was pushing his wheelbarrow full of earth to block off the river Severn and drown the good people. It was a hot day and he was tired when he met a cobbler with a huge sack of boots and shoes on his back. 'How far is it to the Severn?' asked the Evil One. The cobbler suspected him of being up to no good so he said 'Miles and miles. I wore out all these boots and shoes coming from there!' The Devil was horrified and tipped up his wheelbarrow before going off back to Hell. Cam Peak stands there still.

Cam has some fine large houses built from the late medieval period and relatively unspoilt. One of the best, Cam Manor, was destroyed in an accidental fire recently and its site has been built on. There still remains one fine example, The Steps, which has some lovely old traditions and a ghost.

Cam is moving into a new phase in its long history, perhaps for the better of the village as a whole.

Chalford 🐚

The guide books tell us that Chalford is the second largest village in the country. It is often likened to an alpine village because the houses cling to the side of the hill, many accessible only by footpath.

Built in terraces, the village has no centre. Some people moving into the village find this difficult to live with and soon move again. Because Chalford rises from the valley floor to the top of the hill, it is almost two villages, Chalford and Chalford Hill (or as older residents like to call it, Chalford-on-the-Hill).

Industry has always flourished in the valley where the river Frome flows side by side with the Thames & Severn Canal. In fact Chalford is at the end of the Golden Valley which it is believed derived its name from the wealth that the valley made. Modern industry has taken over from the cloth industry which made Chalford great during the 18th and 19th centuries. Many of the large, beautiful Cotswold stone houses in the village belonged to the mill owners and the small cottages that sprang up housed the weavers. Names in the village remind us of its past history in the cloth trade. A small estate called 'The Weavers' and a district named 'Rack Hill' were so called because it was where the finished dyed cloth was dried on racks fitted into the south-facing hillside. It is only in very recent years that any street names were put up in the village upon the insistence of The Fire Brigade. The names were seemingly done in a hurry as many are disappointing for such an unusual village as Chalford.

In the past clever and famous sons of the village include Peter van der Waals, a famous wood craftsman who carried on the tradition of William Morris and Ernest Gimson in a factory in Chalford which closed in 1937. He made furniture for Queen Mary's Doll's House and much of his work is in the Cheltenham Museum although Chalford is fortunate to have some of his work in the Parish Church, Christ Church. Just to mention one piece, the lectern, which is inlaid with mother of pearl, silver and ivory.

The earliest known famous son was Roger Bacon the 13th century scholar and philosopher – he received his early education at St Mary's, another district on the edge of the village where there is now a fine old house and mill. The mill is gradually being restored to a very high standard. St Mary's is also connected with James Bradley (Astronomer Royal) 1692–1762 who married the daughter of the house and died there.

Many of the older folk still talk of the Chalford Feast with awe. It was held in August and lasted a week. It got such a bad reputation that outings were arranged to Weston-super-Mare by the Temperance Society to take their followers and anyone else

44

who wished to get away from 'the goings-on'. Until the First World War there was also an annual feast at the east end of the village at Ashmeads. Today events are much less riotous. The various organisations hold their fetes and coffee-mornings and The Village Hall Project holds an annual fete near The Round House. This house was once a canal lengthman's cottage and then a museum and is now a residence once more and is the landmark for the village.

The Village Hall Project has come about because this huge village does not have a Village Hall and the most popular event it has arranged has become an annual tradition. For one day in the year many people offer their gardens to The Garden Trail where visitors can come not only to admire the gardens but the myriad of views that each garden affords, and tread the paths where not all that long ago the donkeys trod on their way to deliver the bread, milk and other essentials.

Charlton Kings 🦐

The medieval customs of this manor were peculiar. The youngest son was the customary heir and a widow inherited all her husband's property (not the usual one third) for her life and twelve years, so she could raise money on it. The lord of Cheltenham was either the king or a distant monastery, so there was no resident lord and consequently no manor house. There was no resident priest. The advowson of Cheltenham church (of which Charlton was a chapelry) was held by the Canons of Cirencester and served by them.

The chief industry of Charlton Kings used to be farming, both arable and as markets developed, dairy farming. Barley was an important crop used for malting and many pubs made their own beer. Maltsters appear among the more wealthy men of the community. There were the usual village craftsmen; one family, the Cleevelys, have been carpenters and builders since the 17th century. Later there was considerable sand and gravel extraction, and brick-burning. The Black and White Coach Company started here. Today there is still farming and some light industry, but most people work either in Cheltenham or Gloucester. Local shops cater for day to day needs. We have an excellent library and two post offices. These facilities are a blessing because of the large number of homes for the elderly. There are four major places of worship, evening classes, and a vast number of active groups and societies.

The popular Victorian poet Sydney Dobell lived at Detmore, a house to the north of the London Road. This house appears as 'Longfield' in *John Halifax, Gentleman* and is used to illustrate one edition. *Alice through the Looking Glass* probably originated in a visit the real Alice paid to her grandfather, the Rev. H. Liddell at Hetton Lawn. Lewis Carroll came to see her there and the famous looking glass is still in the house. The real Tailor of Gloucester is buried in the local cemetery, but his true story is not a patch on what Beatrix Potter made of it.

In the terrible agricultural depression of the late 19th century, Charlton Kings was badly hit. There was no work for the men. The women kept their families by taking in Cheltenham's washing. Otherwise there was the garden and the family pig. Those pigs have left their mark on building development of that date. They might not be kept within a certain distance of human dwellings. Therefore the houses were laid out with long narrow gardens and piggy lived at the far end. The importance of washing is shown by a bye-law which forbade the lighting of bonfires on Mondays till after six o'clock.

One genuine folk custom which survived till 1939 was that of 'Buff Blowing', a form of wassailing. Very early on New Year's Morning, groups of boys went round the village chanting a rhyme, remembered in several forms:

> Buff blow
> Fare well
> God send
> Ere well,
> Every sprig
> And every spray,
> Apples to roast
> Nuts to crack
> A barrel of cider ready to tap
> Coo-ee (or Shoo-ee or Choo-ee)

Then they hammered on the door, hoping for pence, apples or cake. If the door was not opened quickly, they added 'Old Year Out, New Year In, Choo-ee'.

It is recorded that we once had a summerpole (May pole) in the churchyard but it was forbidden under the Commonwealth. Almost to within living memory we had a traditional troupe of mummers in which the Turkish Knight was metamorphosed into 'The Turkey Snipe'.

As for ghosts and witches, we are free from such follies. How could we have witches? It is impossible to get into the village without crossing running water!

Chedworth 🌿

Attempted murder and an exciting discovery are two dramatic events which have marked Chedworth's history in the past 150 years and by an incredible coincidence, gamekeepers and woods have figured in both.

In 1833, posters in the area announced a £50 reward for the capture of Giles Coates wanted for the attempted murder of a gamekeeper in Chedworth Woods. Giles Coates was a watchmaker, a member of a well-known Chedworth family of clock and watchmakers, who whilst poaching in the woods was disturbed in his clandestine activities by gamekeeper George Simpson. To avoid capture, Coates fired at Simpson and severely injured him. Coates made off to London leaving behind a shot-gun and his hat, but he was re-captured and brought to trial at Gloucester Assizes where he was sentenced to death. Later he was reprieved and transported to Tasmania, but the ship was wrecked and of the 80 convicts on board only one survived and it was not Giles Coates.

Thirty years later, in 1864, an altogether happier event occurred in Chedworth Woods. This time a gamekeeper was digging for his ferret when he noticed fragments of tesserae, the pieces of Roman mosaic. He could never have imagined that his chance discovery would lead to the excavation of one of England's finest Roman Villas, now the property of the National Trust and visited by people from all over the world. This residence of a wealthy Roman merchant, his family and servants with its dining-room, bath houses and hypocaust set in a spectacular wooded valley, would alone make Chedworth worthy of a visit, but the village has much more to offer.

In the Middle Ages the wool of the sheep, the Cotswold Lion, grazing on the Wolds, brought wealth to the area. The magnificent churches are a legacy of that prosperity and an abiding tribute to the skill and craftsmanship of the local masons and builders who created their masterpieces in local stone. The church of St Andrews dates from 1100 and it remained almost unchanged until the fine range of perpendicular windows and the exquisite wine glass pulpit were added in the 15th century. From Saxon times a dwelling has occupied the site adjacent to the church as the present Manor does. It reveals its age in many ways including 3 fireplaces from different ages in its kitchen.

In 1491 when Elizabeth of York, wife of Henry VII came to Chedworth to visit her royal aunts and the newly restored church, the Manor already belonged to her husband. The medieval street, still known as Queen Street, records that historic visit and retains many of its 17th century buildings, including the Seven Tuns Inn.

In 1891 the railway came to the village bringing enormous changes in development and attitudes. Before it fell to Dr Beeching's axe in 1961, this single country track had earned its place in railway history by becoming a vital link in transporting troops to the south coast as the armies of the West assembled for D-Day.

At times it appears that the village has changed beyond recognition, but at other times, as when the Chedworth Silver band, formed in the middle 1800s, plays for the village Fete on the Manor lawn, one can close one's eyes and imagine that time has almost stood still in this beautiful part of Gloucestershire.

Churchdown 🦋

At the turn of the century the population of Churchdown was under 1,000, now it must be one of the largest villages in the country, with a population of over 10,000. Its ancient church of St Bartholomew has stood for 800 years on the top of Chosen Hill, on a site believed to have been occupied by a pagan temple in pre-Christian times. From here, 580 feet above sea level, extensive views can be enjoyed, looking over Gloucester, Cheltenham, the Cotswolds, Malverns and Bredon Hill.

The old church and verger's cottage stood alone on Chosen Hill, alone that is until reservoirs were built by the Water Board who also put in a road which gave motor access to the church and burial ground. Hitherto coffins had to be carried up by bearers and in bad weather by sleigh. Because of this inaccessibility, in 1905 St Andrew's Church was built at the foot of the hill, followed by another church in the new parish of St John. These, together with a Methodist and a Catholic church cater for the spiritual needs of the population.

After the First World War an Ex-Service Men's Club was built in the centre of the village, now the Churchdown Club. When in 1924 the early members decided they wanted bowling greens and tennis courts they were in for a shock. They purchased the land for £200 and then it became a do-it-yourself job. A working party started digging and soon came upon a large number of skeletons. Further investigation revealed what appeared to be a mass grave, with several layers of skeletons, but no funeral furniture or coffin nails. The Archaeology Society came to investigate. Skeletons of both sexes with no injuries ruled out the battle theory and it is strongly believed that, way back in the 14th century when England was ravaged by the Black Death, Churchdown suffered with the rest of the country.

Today, Churchdown is very much a dormitory area for Cheltenham and Gloucester but despite its size it has managed to retain its village atmosphere.

The 'Home Basket' was devised by a Churchdown lady and has now spread to other parts of the country – a scheme similar to the hospital trolley shop but for the elderly and housebound, when perhaps the regular visit is looked forward to almost as much as the 'goodies' in the basket.

Altogether Churchdown is a very desirable village to live in with easy access to Cheltenham and Gloucester for shopping and the cultural activities they provide.

Coalway 🌿

Because Coalway is, and always has been a caring community, many of its inhabitants can recall memories of a bygone era in splendid detail. Quite a lot of people are related to each other, and also, it seems are a grandchild to someone who owned a shop, or who was a coal miner, or even was taught by one of the local characters.

Take for example the toll-keeper, who can be seen on an old print of 1888, with a small child beside her. She was called Miss Gleed, and was known to have given sewing lessons to the young girls of Coalway, and when a passer-by or traveller called out, she would leave her pupils, and take the toll money, and open the five barred gate that crossed the road, that led down to Parkend. Sadly, in 1888, the need for tolls was abolished, but all over the forest you can still find the quaint, hexagonal pike houses.

Life in the Forest of Dean has revolved around coal-mining, and in and around Coalway, there are plenty of walks and nature trails, all of which will take you past a digging or the leftover scar of a hopeful mine. Coal had been mined in the Forest for centuries, and by the 18th century there was a proliferation of pits. But it was the 19th century which saw the advent of the large collieries: Crump Meadow, Foxes Bridge, Lightmoor, New Bowson, New Fancy, Trafalgar, Waterloo. By 1900 the annual output of coal from the Forest was one million tons and it was estimated that there were 300 million tons of unworked coal, most of it winnable, in Dean.

In 1874 there were five thousand colliers in the Forest, and by 1920, there were seven thousand, but many of the colliers were sometimes only working one or two shifts per week. In 1955 the number had reduced to two and a half thousand, and ten years later the last big colliery was closed.

Poignantly, there are people today who can remember their fathers or uncles and brothers, making their way on grey misty mornings to the pits, wearing caps and scarves and hobnailed boots and moleskin trousers, with yorks tied just below their knees. They would carry their Tommy bags of food, and cans for water or cold tea, and swing their carbide lamps, in a procession that made them look like a string of pearls. When they got down into the pit, they would strip down to their singlet, trousers and boots, and hack away at the unyielding black gold, with only a skullcap for protection.

Nevertheless, there are also lovely recollections of the blacksmith Mr Morgan, who had his smithy near to the Toll house. His premises, with its half double doors, was a great attraction on cold days, when the local youngsters would hang over the bottom door and watch while the smith shaped the horseshoes. It was a treat if you were allowed inside to watch.

The best memories though, seem to have come out of the many get-togethers that were arranged through the local Pisgah Chapel, or the Sunday School, when families really enjoyed themselves, and at events like Cherry Fair held up at Nagshead Lodge you would spend most of the summer day picking the fruit, and then filling the baskets and your tummy. Then if you had any energy left, you joined in the fun and games, and what sports days they had! Girls looked forward to these times because they could wear their new frock or hat. Talking of which, there was the big black hat that Grandma wore on Sundays to Chapel, and she would sit so straight in the pew, and you would sit behind and long to touch her fur coat or the fox stole around her shoulders.

But the 1926 pit strike brought with it some bad memories and sad times, but Coalway like any other little village similar to it, rallied round and together the families would do what they could to help each other, like going to Broadwell for free dinners, or your father cutting hair or mending shoes to earn a few extra shillings. The children also did their jobs to help the money go round, and each day before school or after, they would go off to the woods, and scrabble around gathering sticks and blocks for the winter supply, or cut sufficient supplies of fern or bracken for the fowls' winter nests.

Coalway, in the Forest of Dean still is a close community. There always is a smile and a wave, and an enquiry as to your well-being. The corner shop is still a gathering place to catch up on the local gossip, as well as to get your provisions. We've lost the Pike House and the Pit, and a few other landmarks, but a walk around the Forest near to the Management Training Centre of the Forestry Commission will soon awaken memories of a bygone era.

Compton Abdale ✥

There is a crocodile in the Cotswolds. Yes, truly, in the Square at Compton Abdale, just a mile south of the A40. He spouts water, most beautiful spring water, into a huge stone trough which we used regularly for drinking before 'the mains' came to the village. Our crocodile is not our only beastie though – come on a mini-safari one day and find all our other creatures. They are to be found nowhere else.

One of the oldest houses in the village has most unusual chimney-pots with little flat roofs and on one of them sits a tiny stone bird looking for all the world like a sparrow, so much so that you wait for him to move or fly away. There is also a little bird atop a wrought iron gate but, not unexpectedly, the church yields most finds.

On the tower itself, below the golden weather-cock, there are four pinnacles, one at each corner formed like bears holding staffs (or are they wolves?!). Beneath them, on the sides of the tower are several marvellous gargoyles, some with their original lead spouts in their mouths.

The church is named for St Oswald and he is also to be found on the outside of the tower blowing a trumpet, but if you go around to the back of the church you can find traces of our Pagan ancestry. Above a window you will see our Green Man, peering out from among the leaves. Maybe the stone masons carved him there just to play safe! While you are at the rear of the church look for another little bird, in cement this time, perched by the defunct boiler-room chimney.

There are yet more creatures to be found inside the church

including a beautifully carved eagle whose wings form the lectern. St George is killing the dragon on a wall painting which, sadly, was damaged when it was discovered and there is also a very cheeky little devil on the wall back by the belfry.

If you are lucky enough to visit the church when our special altar cloth is in use you can add to your score of creatures very easily. This altar cloth was designed and made by members of the congregation, men and women alike; the work gave us much enjoyment and a great sense of achievement when it was completed. Every flower, leaf and insect was made separately and then fixed to the backing material. The butterflies and flowers are those to be found in the area but do not miss all the ladybirds. Also, if you look very carefully you will find pieces of embroidered honey-comb with visiting bees.

All the bells in the tower have recently been re-tuned and re-hung and we now have a new ringing chamber.

Compton Abdale lies in a deep hollow among the Cotswold hills and running into it are several U-shaped dry valleys. This proves that they were formed by the action of glaciers during the last Ice Age. We have a brook which gurgles through the village and is one of the tiny tributaries which form the head-waters of the river Thames.

There are plenty of good old houses to be seen in the village, both large and small and some sympathetic conversion and new buildings, too. A water-mill at Compton was mentioned in the Domesday Book and the present old building is being converted to a dwelling house, altering the outside as little as possible. Much of the original machinery is still in situ including the large water-wheel at the rear. This was fed by water from two connecting small ponds nearby, where there are always coot and moorhen to be seen, and sometimes herons too.

Cranham 🦋

The wealth of Cranham and its beauty lie in the woods. Samuel Rudder in 1779 mentions the beech woods with their timber and charcoal which were sent to Birmingham for the manufacture of gunstocks. Pottery was made from the time of Queen Elizabeth, and even, it is claimed, from Roman times.

Otherwise the main occupation was farming. The chief farms were at Overtown or Upper town, Haregrove or Undertown, Woodside and Freams. There were no manors or titles in Cranham. The Pinching family claimed to have owned several farms and much land, but lost them when they backed the Royalists in the Civil War. The Horlick family occupied several cottages and it is said that the recipe for malted milk was evolved by the housewives seeking to make a baby-food. The family spread from Cranham, some emigrated to America where they made a fortune and returned to settle in Cowley Manor. There is a tomb of Sir Alexander Horlick J.P. in Cranham churchyard (died 1889).

Of the Pinching family there are a few tombs. There is also a ghost, a little lady in grey who still moves around the places they once occupied. The other ghost is now old enough to have come to rest, Idel or Eddel the Saxon leader who was buried at Idel's tump behind the Royal William and used to haunt Eddel's Lane.

A famous visitor to the village was Gustav Holst who sometimes played the harmonium in the church. He stayed at Midwinter Cottage and composed the tune *Cranham* to the words of *In the bleak midwinter*.

A benefactor to the village was J. H. Edwards of Woodside who presented the children's playing field. He also bought and renovated Riching's Pottery and presented it to the County Scout Association for their headquarters.

A few years ago Jo Henson of the Rare Breeds Society presented Cranham Feast Committee with a few specimens of real old Cotswold Sheep which are bred and kept at Batch Farm.

Colonel James Carne VC, DSO, DL who commanded the 1st Battalion of The Gloucestershire Regiment at the battle of the Imjin River in the Korean war was a resident of Cranham.

A new name has been added to the recent Ordnance map, Gladys's Leap, below Haregrove. This is to commemorate Gladys Hillier who for thirty-five years faithfully delivered the post and had to follow a footpath that crossed a brook.

Cranham Feast takes place on the second Monday in August and is part of the Patronal Feast of St James the Greater. The central theme is a Mime commemorating the meeting of the Squire and his tenants. Deer are roasted. There is a boundary race to represent the ancient beating of the bounds. Local tug-of-war teams compete and there is a week-end of cricket, sports, a luncheon and a dance. Combined with a Fun Fair this attracts huge crowds such as could never have been imagined when it was revived in 1951.

When Cheltenham was becoming a fashionable spa, a popular outing was a drive up through Leckhampton and Birdlip to Cranham Woods where an enterprising Mr Todd had built a Swiss Cottage. Here were beautiful gardens, fishponds and facilities for archery and refreshments. At the end of the 19th century three Cheltenham doctors recognising the attractive site founded a sanatorium and later moved to Cranham Lodge nearby. This venture flourished for many years, becoming one of the most successful and luxurious private hospitals. Patients came from far and near and included Owen Nares, George Orwell, Kenneth Hare, and James Elroy Flecker who wrote:

> 'Have I not chased the fluting Pan
> Through Cranham's sober trees?'

Many people from the village worked in the sanatorium and gardens until the decline in tuberculosis and the introduction of the National Health Service caused its closure in 1956, and nothing remains now except the doctor's house and the name Sanatorium Road.

In July 1788 George III with his Queen and some of his children drove up to Birdlip and Cranham from the village of Cheltenham. An old woman, unaware of his identity came from her cottage and presented the old gentleman and his lady with a dish of fragrant woodland strawberries, which was graciously accepted and soon cleared. The old woman stood by and curtsied when the dish was handed back with thanks. 'You be mortal welcome' she said, 'but I don't know who you be – the Squire I s'pose?' 'No, my good woman, I have left my picture on the dish.' When she put the empty plate upon the table and saw the golden guinea glittering, she realised she had seen the King, 'good old Varmer George'.

Down Hatherley

Mentioned in the Domesday book the village of Down Hatherley is a sprawling one. The oldest part is built along the Down

Hatherley Lane and around the church, whilst the newer section is built along the main Gloucester to Tewkesbury road.

The village history goes back to Saxon times, Hatherley Court being the main estate in the village, a property that Oliver Cromwell knocked about a bit.

It was the home of Sir Mathew Wood who was once Lord Mayor of London. He founded the village school and left many charities to the village folk. In years gone by the court has always been the focal point of the village, with its Cromwellian staircase and panelled rooms. Many a village fete and children's party has been held on its vast lawns. But alas it's now a hotel, much to the village's dismay, and its Saxon moat has now been filled in.

Most of the large houses in the village are near the church. The rectory, a fine house, is now turned into flats, Woodfold cottage is the home of Mr N. Peria who is our local author. The Jones's have farmed Hatherley Farm for many years. Ash Lane is made up of homes built of First World War army huts.

The owners of these properties moved out of Gloucester Westend area to live in the country and work the land around the wooden bungalows they had built. The church was originally Norman but was rebuilt and only the tower is original. The font is all lead, and is very much treasured because there are only two of this type of font in the country.

One of the past rectors was Rev. Button Ciwinett whose son signed the America's Treaty of Independence in 1776. In later years the rectors have searched high and low for any signature of Button Ciwinitt junior because the Americans would pay heavily for such a signature, and the Down Hatherley church would have no further financial worries. But it has been stated, that, at the time the church was so disgusted with Button Ciwinett for signing the declaration that they burnt everything belonging to him in the parish.

We are very lucky to have our own hall, built in 1932. It is still used very much, for all kinds of village events and society meetings.

Down Hatherley village tries to keep its identity of being very rural just 3 miles from Gloucester and 6 miles from Cheltenham. It is hoped that the village fete, the cricket matches, church gift days, afternoon teas in some lovely garden will continue as part of village life in years to come.

Dumbleton 🌿

The village is a contented mixture of old Dumbleton families and newer arrivals who have moved in over the last twenty years or so to houses built on land sold by the Dumbleton Estate. There are a few council houses and old people's bungalows.

The Hall is owned by the Post Office Fellowship of Remembrance (their War Memorial) and run by them as a holiday centre open all the year round. The present hall was built in the 1820s by Edward Holland who was one of the founders of the Royal Agricultural College at Cirencester, and a cousin of Mrs Elizabeth Gaskell. Mrs Gaskell visited Dumbleton and her daughter Marianne married Edward's eldest son, Thurston. On Edward's death the property was sold to the Eyres family, later Eyres-Monsell. It was Lady Monsell who sold it to the Post Office in 1959. The park with its beautiful trees remains the property of the Dumbleton Estate.

The Hall, as might be expected, has its ghost. A grey lady has been seen mounting the stairs by the staff in recent times. But the real village ghost seems to be a white lady who walks round the fish pond by the cricket field at midnight and then across what is now Garden Close. Several older villagers recall how frightened they used to be of her in their youth.

The cricket club's setting must be one of the loveliest anywhere. The club celebrated its centenary in 1985. Its most famous member was Vic Hopkins who kept wicket for Gloucestershire and played in 139 matches for the county between 1934 and 1948.

The land above the Hall is let as a shoot. The gamekeeper, Brian Wells, is a notable sportsman who has shot clay pigeons for England at least a dozen times, several as Captain. He won the European Championship in 1977 and in 1978 was runner-up in the first World Championship. He has appeared on television with his father, gamekeeper before him, talking on clay pigeon shooting and his father, Bernard, has been seen talking on the life of a gamekeeper.

Well-known too, but in bell ringing circles, is Fred Nurden. The Rector's son while ringing bells in Yorkshire was asked where his home was. On being told the questioner immediately asked 'How's Fred Nurden?' Fred, now in his eighties has rung bells all his life and is a 'College Youth'. He has a fund of stories and a tongue which still keeps order on practice night. Dumbleton's bells, cast as a single peal in 1729, are said to be the sweetest in Gloucestershire.

The Duntisbournes ༄

An Anglo-Saxon chieftain called Dunt who lived in Brimpsfield gave his name to the stream or bourne which runs through the Duntisbourne valley. It is a small stream, rising near Winston and joining the Churn at Stratton on the outskirts of Cirencester, a distance of about five miles. The four villages of the Duntisbournes are strung along the river. At the head is Duntisbourne Abbotts and then Duntisbourne Leer, both of which are contained in the parish of Duntisbourne Abbotts. About a mile from Leer is Middle Duntisbourne and then Duntisbourne Rous.

The histories of these parishes are typical of small rural communities in England. There were the Lords of the Manor who owned the land, the Rectors, the yeoman and tenant farmers, and the landless farm workers. Until the 19th century Abbotts and Leer did not have a Lord of the Manor resident in the village, and Rous has never had one at all. The Rectors, from the time of the Reformation until the mid-19th century, were frequently absent from their livings and the churches suffered greatly from neglect and decay.

After the Reformation, Leer was acquired by the Pleydell family of Ampney Park and remained in that family until the end of the 19th century. Abbotts had a number of different Lords of the Manor until it also was acquired by the Pleydells in the mid 18th century.

The Pleydells do not seem to have concerned themselves greatly with the villages in all this time. Administration of parish affairs was in the hands of the Manor Court who dealt with minor misdemeanours and the regulation of agricultural practices. In the 18th century the Overseers of the Poor kept accounts in both parishes. These show that problem families are not just a 20th century phenomenon. In 1737 one Collins was forcibly kept in custody in Abbotts and made to marry the mother of their illegitimate child. In Rous in 1765 and for the next 30 years

Barbara Coates and her family were regularly helped with payments of rent and with supplies of wood, clothing and shoes. Barbara seems to have had a number of illegitimate children and a daughter or grand-daughter of hers, Sara Coates, was convicted in 1810 of stealing some clothes from her employer and sentenced to be hanged.

Life in Abbotts and Leer seems to have improved in the 19th century with the coming of Abbotts' most distinguished inhabitant, Dr Matthew Baillie, to Duntisbourne House. Dr Baillie was a royal physician and attended George III through the long years of his mental illness. He was one of the most outstanding doctors of his day and regarded his attendance on the king as a tiresome duty – and charged accordingly. In 1812 his fee was over £3,500. Dr Baillie used Duntisbourne House first as a country retreat and then retired to the village, becoming the epitome of a Cotswold squire. When he died in 1823 his son continued the tradition until his death at the great age of 98 in 1894.

Church life in the early 19th century was at a particularly low ebb and the Dissenters became active in both villages. One of the most remarkable was Elizabeth Cross of Cotswold Farm who, with her husband, set up a mission school on the Pacific island of Tonga. They converted the then King and Queen of Tonga to Christianity and the Tonga royal family has been Methodist ever since. Sadly, Mrs Cross and her husband were shipwrecked on their way to Fiji and she died of exposure on a raft.

Now, most people are commuters or retired; the houses and cottages are improved and extended and the villages are probably better kept now than at any time in their history. The Victorian regime of squire and rector ruling the villages has gone for ever. The population of the valley is smaller, there are no schools or shops and, with most households owning a car, the people of the valley are more outward-looking for work and for entertainment.

Dymock 🌿

A lively and attractive village today, it is well known for its profusion of wild daffodils blooming in the spring. Dymock has many attractions, being surrounded by the Dymock Woods, close to one of the few commercial British vineyards, a butterfly farm – to mention but a few.

Just before the First World War Dymock was the meeting place for many of the eminent poets of the day, Lascelles Abercrombie, Wilfred Gibson, Edward Thomas, John Drinkwater and Rupert Brooke were living in the area. They were joined by Robert Frost, the already well established American bard. It was from Dymock that Abercrombie published the first issue of *New Numbers* – a quarterly magazine aimed at publishing new poetry. This plan was unfortunately not to materialise, due to the onset of the First World War. The famous *War Sonnets* were produced for one of the editions of *New Numbers*.

Another feature of the village, though perhaps not of the aesthetic quality of the Poets, is the treacle mine. A rare characteristic usually in evidence only on the auspicious date of April 1st in favourable years!!

The church of St Mary the Virgin is a haven for historians. The churchyard, too, has its interests – an avenue of lime trees marks the course of the original Roman road, and for the collector of epitaphs the following will surely amuse:

'Too sweeter babes yeun nare did see Than God
amitly give to Wee
But they were ortaken wee ague fits and here
they lives as dead as Wits.'

Eastcombe

Eastcombe must have seen more changes in the last decade than any other village in Gloucestershire. Wedged between the two villages a vast estate is springing up – the Manor Estate. When completed it will consist of more than 900 houses of varying shapes, sizes and prices. All this on fields that were full of wildlife of every description, including the brown hare and hundreds of skylarks.

In 'the good old days' everyone knew each other and lived in the same houses or cottages all their lives. A certain amount of in-breeding resulted in some odd characters. A fellow with a frightful squint carrying a bundle and probably tapping at a gate hoping to find a loose spar would ask 'Doo oooh know ower Annie – ower Annie is mye seester?' – that was 'ower Freddie'. These two managed to survive on parish relief to quite an old age. One old dear – 'batty as a brush' – spent whole nights banging on zinc and giving her neighbours sleepless hours. Another character known as 'Queen Bess' always dressed in black and carried a huge black brolly to chase away the teasing children. Most cottagers kept a pig or chickens. 'Queen Bess' kept chickens. One spring the 'broody' yielded twelve chicks instead of the expected baker's dozen. 'Queen Bess' took the thirteenth egg to bed and it hatched out in her bosom!

Eastcombe, being virtually cut off from the 'outside world', was noted for its lawlessness and there are tales of murders and consequent hauntings. Some of the very old were carried over the hill to end their days in Stroud workhouse although one 'local' tells the tale of how his great-grandfather got to the top of the hill with his father, sat the old chap on the stile, looked at him, and carried him home again!

The Toadsmoor Valley, originally Todsmoor or Valley of the Foxes, runs through Bismore, Kitlye, Cricketty and Nashend to Bisley and is flanked by Maccus, Hawkley and Baker's Woods. The old meadows are alive with the flowers and fauna of yester-year, having escaped the blight of insecticides and pesticides. The stream rising from Bisley's Seven Springs flows through the valley, under the Swilley Bridge, past Cutham's Stile, through the Withey Bed and into Toadsmoor Lake, with tales of hauntings on the way! The dawn chorus is music to any ornithologist's ear.

To the west of the valley lies Lypiatt Park where five gardeners and many estate workers were employed at the turn of the century. Sadly today many of the gardens have disappeared and buildings are decaying – a reflection of the modern era. All the cottages in the hamlet of Bismore and many in Eastcombe were part of Lypiatt Park Estate and when it was dispersed cottagers were given the opportunity of buying their homes at knockdown prices. Two families, namely the Pillings and the Nobeses bought theirs – at a later date it transpired that they had bought each others! Without estate workers footpaths have become overgrown or non-existent. Many horseriders use the woods and help to keep these paths open.

Westward from Lypiatt stand the Middle Lypiatt farms and Nether Lypiatt Manor, belonging to Prince Michael of Kent and known locally as 'the Haunted House'. Long ago an owner of the house named Judge Coxe sentenced a blacksmith to death for stealing sheep. The offender was offered a reprieve if he made a pair of wrought iron gates for the manor within a given time. This he did but there was a minor mistake on one of the gates and he was duly hanged. His ghost is said to gallop thrice round the courtyard on a white horse!

Formerly Eastcombe villagers went to the Stroud Valley for their employment but today many commute to Cheltenham, Gloucester, Bristol, Bath and Oxford.

Despite the growing and changing population the community spirit still exists.

Eastington ❦

Eastington may not be the most beautiful village but it has a long history, being first mentioned around 1085, according to A. E. Keys *History of Eastington*, although Alkerton, the central part of the village, was at that time the more important place (then spelt 'Alcryntone').

In 1220 Eastington was mentioned as 'Eadstan's tun', meaning Eadstan's farm or settlement and since then seems to have taken over from Alkerton.

Parts of a Roman settlement have been discovered at Westend but this has never been fully explored.

The Duke of Buckingham, cousin to Henry VIII, owned property in Gloucestershire, and was a benefactor to the Parish Church. The church has a Norman font and a pre-Reformation monumental brass.

The Manor House, now no longer in existence, was situated to the west of the church, and was the home of the Stephens family, one of whose members was a signatory to the death-sentence on King Charles I. For this act, it was said, the family was cursed, and has now died out.

Early this century people were mainly occupied in agriculture and the cloth trade but now travel further afield to more diversified categories of employment.

One Rector, the Reverend Sidney Rimmer, in the late 19th century, became so unpopular that his effigy was burned as a protest.

In more recent times, other personalities have been the Reverend G. T. A. Ward, Rector for over 30 years, a musician, scholar, engineer and printer, also Mr Charles Hooper, owner of Bonds Mill (cloth mill) together with members of the de Lisle Bush family of Eastington Park.

Until about 20 years ago May Day was a great feature of village life, when the children would parade round the village performing country-dancing in honour of their May Queen. Mr J. W. Rowbotham, the headmaster of the school for around 30 years, instituted this and it continued for some years after he left to take Holy Orders.

Since the Second World War the village has almost doubled in size.

Many village organisations hold their meetings in the Village Hall, which was built on land given by the late James Warner and helped by donations from the de Lisle Bush family.

Ebrington

Ebrington, affectionately known to local people as 'Yubberton' is a quiet little village two miles or so to the north and east of Chipping Campden, in the northernmost tip of Gloucestershire, close to the Warwickshire border. Its abundant supplies of spring water encouraged settlements in the area long before the Roman occupation, and throughout the centuries the history of Ebrington has been bound up with that of the land. Even today, when so many small towns and villages are experiencing the effects of rural depopulation, those ties remain strong. Ebrington does have a sprinkling of holiday homes and, in recent years, an increasing number of newcomers have settled in the village, but it has managed to absorb all these quite happily without losing its basic identity, that of a community which lives and works upon the land.

Ebrington is one of those villages which, for some reason or another, became the butt of local humour and many a tale is told of the 'Yubberton Yawnies' or simpletons. If these were ever true,

however, let no one imagine that they characterise the village of today, which manages to convey the impression of a small but enterprising community determined to meet the challenges of the latter half of the 20th century. Perhaps the ability to take and recount jokes against itself indicates a certain strength of character which has always underlain any appearances to the contrary.

The Yubberton folk, it is said, wanted it always to be summer and so they let the hedges grow tall to keep the cuckoo in! Then, because they were jealous of the fine tower at Chipping Campden, the Yubberton Yawnies manured their church tower.

> 'Master Keyte, a man of great power
> Lent 'em a cart to muck the tower
> And when the muck began to sink
> They swore the tower had grown an inch.'

Sometimes they managed to get their own back, as shown in the tale of the traveller who asked the landlord of the Ebrington Inn where he was. On being told he exclaimed 'Oh, Ebrington, that be where all the fools live!' to which the landlord retorted 'Well I don't know that all live here. We get plenty passing through.'

And in a sense, it would indeed be a foolish traveller who merely 'passed through', for although Ebrington may lie off the main tourist track, time spent exploring its quiet byways would be well worthwhile. No traveller should neglect a visit to the church, dedicated to a Saxon, St Eadburga, which has a fine Norman arch and several interesting monuments, including ones to Sir John Fortescue and William Keyte, who bequeathed the Cow Charity in 1632, providing for '. . . the Milk of Ten Good Milch Kine to be distributed from the Tenth of May to the First of November in Perpetuity . . .' to be given to the poor of Ebrington. The Charity is still administered today, although ever since the Second World War when shortages and changes in agricultural policy led to difficulties over the provision of milk, payments have been made in money.

Edge ❦

Popular with the Gloucester gentry in the 19th century as a venue for country outings, and renowned nowadays for its snowdrop-carpeted churchyard, the village of Edge straddles the hilltop between Brookthorpe and Pitchcombe on the A4173 road. On early maps the name Rudge is shown to the east and it was part of the Edge tithing of Painswick.

It is an ecclesiastical district formed in 1873 from parts of four neighbouring parishes and covers a wide area of farmland woods and commons, home of some rare wild flowers and butterflies. It contains about one hundred houses, some modern and others dating back to the 15th century. The majority of the inhabitants are commuters or retired with some individual craftsmen, agriculture being the main industry. The village shop, school and post office have all closed.

In 1866 the owner of Harescombe Grange, finding the journey to Harescombe Church rather difficult requested a church be built at Edge at an easier walking distance. It stands at the crossing of an old Roman ridge road from Bath through Paganhill to Gloucester Eastgate, and the Stroud–Gloucester turnpike road. The armies of Edward IV marched along the ridgeway in 1471 to the battle of Tewkesbury, probably camping on Huddiknoll Hill.

To the west of the church lies Stockend, once a hamlet of ill-repute according to Henry Warren who was inspired whilst living there to write *A Cotswold Year*. In it he describes a neighbour, a very colourful character, much addicted to home-made wine, who in later years died tragically after downing a bottle of carbolic acid, mistaking it for wine. An ancient deerpark once covered the fields below the National Trust beechwoods, near the site of a Roman villa probably the farmstead for the camp on Haresfield Hill. The ghost of a Roman centurion is said to haunt the area reputedly seen by a Whiteshill policeman. Perhaps those earlier mischievous choirboys, white surplices spread, jumping out at dusk on unsuspecting passers-by gave the place an eerie reputation.

Beyond the church is Horsepools, an estate now divided, which was once owned by the Maitland family. One of its members married into the Darwin family, bringing the famous monkeys to Little Horsepools, fascinating many a passer-by. Seven-Leaze Lane runs to Spoonbed and Painswick Beacon over Huddiknoll Hill, where in 1644 Cavaliers and Roundheads fought a pitched battle. The latter were forced to retreat down a steep and narrow lane towards Brookthorpe, where helmets and skeletons were found buried in 1855 some local folk using the helmets for coal-scuttles.

This lane passes behind Harescombe Grange where Beatrix Potter spent several holidays when writing her children's stories.

A huge oak tree still stands on Edge Farm. It is over 800 years old and the trunk, now hollow, measures ten feet in diameter. Nearby is a field called Hanging Hill, and the legend goes that a farmhand wagered to mow the whole of it in one day, and failing, hanged himself. An eerie swishing noise at night is said to be the sound of the grass falling from his scythe as he tries to finish his task.

Hilles, a mansion built by Detmar Blow, once Lord of the Manor of Painswick, overlooks Gloucester. He was a friend of William Morris, and Rudyard Kipling spent holidays there. The roof was originally thatched with Norfolk reeds which caught fire, lighting the night-sky for miles around. A house at nearby Holcombe has a cellar reached by an underground passage, containing a pit once used for illegal cock-fighting.

Towards the Stroud end of the village is Highcroft, a house where Max Beerbohm stayed during the Second World War. It stands near the Edgemoor Inn, formerly the Gloucester House, which greatly extended, caters for many travellers, thus helping to keep alive the old-established attraction to visitors, characteristic of the village of Edge.

Elmore 🌿

The population of Elmore is approximately 220 but past Electoral Rolls reveal that at one time it boasted of 400 and more. These were the days when the men were sea-farers or worked on Elmore Estate or manual work on the farms. With mechanisation many left the village to seek work elsewhere. Today seventy-five per cent of the working inhabitants commute to the city for employment. Some have their own business – including builders, an upholsterer and transport lorries.

About a mile from the boundary of Elmore lies Elmore Court, the home of the Guise family which has held estates in this county from the early days of the 13th century. It would seem that a relative of John de Burgh married Nicholas, son of Robert Guyse and the lady received as a gift from John de Burgh the manor of Elmore.

At the entrance to the Court is a magnificent set of Baroque iron gates surmounted by the heraldic crest of the Guise Family – a swan rising from a ducal coronet. The architecture of the house is a combination of Elizabethan, late Stuart and Georgian styles and the house is open to the public during the summer months on the first Sunday of the month or by appointment.

At the extreme end of the village for some obscure reason which no one seems to be able to explain, one finds the church dedicated to St John the Baptist. It was consecrated by the Bishop of Worcester in July 1315. It contains many monuments to the Guise family but no other special antiquities. The registers which are interesting date from 1779 to 1876. The belfry contains six bells which are rung on special occasions. Two ancient chests, one of oak and one of elm, seven feet long, are to be found in the west end of the church and probably housed the vestments.

The land in Elmore is very fertile and is rich in fauna and flora. With the draining of the meadows however, many species of flowers disappeared including the Snake's Head Fritillary, but as soon as winter shows any sign of slackening, celandines, primroses, cowslips, snowdrops and bluebells herald the spring. The grey squirrel can be seen even on the coldest day and old Brock has his sett up in the woods and takes a nightly stroll down the hill, across the road into the copse beyond to forage for worms. Pheasants, woodpeckers, tomtits, blue-tits, goldfinches, thrushes, robins, wrens, magpies, rooks and crows abound but the blue flash of the kingfisher has long disappeared. At the back of Elmore Court there is a heronry and the return of the herons is awaited and monitored by many.

Throughout the centuries the river Severn has played an important role in the life of the inhabitants of Elmore. Once there were three inns on its banks where the boats used to pull in when they were going from Sharpness to Gloucester. Now there is no public house in the village. In the past the stretch of river at Elmore Back saw active salmon fishing. Today, in late February, March and April countless numbers of people come elver fishing, but since they are bought for export a meal of elvers has now become an expensive luxury.

The stretch of river from Elmore Back to the Stonebench Inn provides an excellent stand for viewing the Severn Bore. Every tide has a bore, but it is in the Spring and Autumn tides that the spectacular wall of water and its spray draw hundreds of visitors from far and wide to witness this strange feature due to the bottle-neck shape of the river.

Stories are told that 'The Shark' — one of the past inns on the Severn was a smugglers' den. The contraband was supposed to be taken across the meadows to what is now No. 1 Spring Lane and hidden under the floor of the house. Not so long back, when some alterations were carried out to the house an underground cellar was discovered so maybe there is some truth in the stories.

For many years Elmore has been spoken of as a dying village, but it is very much alive. What it lacks in amenities is more than compensated in its happy, friendly, community spirit.

Fairford 🦎

Jumbles, variously called rummage — or more grandly Nearly New — sales have become so much a part of every community's calendar that it is difficult to imagine what one did with the 'kept-for-evers' that no longer fit or the odd things that have lost the purpose of their ever being. And however did the local amateur dramatics costume their cast before the days of jumbles?

Well, if you had lived in Fairford before the Second World War shattered the social order of our settled communities, the answer to these problems would have been solved by Fly-O-Gert.

Fly-O-Gert belonged to that special generation of characters which has passed into local folk-lore along with the knife-grinder and the hedgerow-peg gipsies, the paraffin-man and the cheap-jack.

Fly-O-Gert earned her name by being 'fly' — Gert was an endearment. A swarthy, raw-boned woman of indeterminate age, hung around with dangling jewellery of inestimable value — rough-cut diamonds twinkling among the fairground finery — Fly-O-Gert flew along the streets and in and out of homes plying her trade, her whole business housed in a battered suitcase and transported on an equally battered bicycle.

The grinding crunch of bike brakes outside a cottage door heralded the arrival of Gert. From the depths of the striped-paper and mould-spotted lined case would be extracted 'a real bargain, Missus, just right for your Annie I thought — her off to service next week as I understood, and her wanting to look smart-like and you hitting a rough patch with your man on the club as I heard. Better is he now? Ah, well takes time and a drop of ol' Tod's'. (Tod was the chemist who mixed up the same elixir for any and all complaints – in different sized bottles.)

After regaling the potential customer with sound advice – also second-hand – and the suitability of the dress which she had procured specially with Annie in mind, with the usual warranty that she knew 'where it come from', the transaction was completed and another commenced. For by the time Missus had rattled the precious pennies out of the tea-caddy which was the stronghold of the family's emergency fund for 'rainy days', Gert had been 'fly' enough to assess the potential value of the Crown Derby plate on the sideboard. Missus was happy – Annie would be rigged out decent in a dress that could have been one of the gentry's – although protocol prevented Gert from *actually* saying so; true, she was a pretty plate the poorer but had been assured it was going to a good home.

The bartering and bargaining over the old battered suitcase then gave way to Gert's book, for Fly-O-Gert became an agent for the first of the mail order firms to penetrate the home market.

It was never quite the same, though. The foresight and sharp-witted astuteness, the sense of secrecy and intrigue and mystery were shut inside the travel-worn suitcase as her monopoly slipped away with the increase in the mail order business to the homes themselves.

Fly-O-Gert eventually joined her old departed cronies – no doubt she still has a little side-line going with second-hand celestial harp-strings.

Forthampton

Forthampton, three miles from Tewkesbury is bounded by the river Severn on the east, the Worcestershire boundary on the north and west, and Chaceley village on the south. The population is just over 150 and is largely farmed and the village has had little development during this century, only seven houses having been built during the last 100 years. The whole area is attractive, despite the loss of the elms, through having wide grass verges with no

71

curbs, and there are spinneys in many parts between the verges and adjacent fields. There is not a street lamp anywhere! The village's recorded history goes back to the reign of William the Conqueror, being listed as Fortemeltone in Domesday Book 1086.

Forthampton Court was the residence of abbots of Tewkesbury Abbey and alterations have been carried out through the centuries. The building contains the magnificent Banqueting Hall of 1380, the Abbots Chapel and a 13th century picture on wood of Edward the Confessor and the Pilgrim. In 1539 at the time of the Dissolution of the Monasteries, Henry VIII took possession and gave John Wakeman, the last Abbot of Tewkesbury Abbey, the Court as his residence, having appointed him to be the first Bishop of Gloucester. Since the death of Wakeman in 1549 many illustrious families have been in occupation of the building including Earls of Salisbury and Middlesex, and for the last 230 years descendants of the Earl of Hardwicke. John Sarne Yorke, the present occupant and Lord of the Manor is the eighth generation of the family.

The village has a number of timber-framed thatched houses originally with wattle and daub but now with brick infilling. One of these is Brewer's Cottage for many years a bakery, and opposite is Vine Farm of the 16th century with close-set studding, overhanging gable and cruck rear.

The Sanctuary formerly called St Robert, visited by pilgrims in the 13th century on their way to Hereford, has a hall (now filled in with an upper storey) with carved wooden bosses in the ceiling, one boss displaying the arms of the Earls of Gloucester. Records of 1542 show there was a chapel and dovecote.

The church of St Mary is an ancient building of stone, much altered over the centuries. The tower is early 13th century with massive diagonal west buttresses. In 1847 when the village population was almost 500 the north aisle was added. The most interesting feature of the church is the stone altar. It is one of only three which survived in situ at the time of the Reformation of 1538.

The Village Hall was built in the 1870s by Mr John R. Yorke, JP, MP, as a Church of England School, and after functioning for about seventy years became redundant and was then taken over for use as the Village Hall.

In 1793 the Bishop of Gloucester gave a large house near the top of Church Lane to be used as a work house or 'a house of industry' as it was then called. When this ceased to function the building was pulled down and in 1905 a wooden building was erected on the site to be used as the Forthampton Working Men's Club. It is in full service to this day.

The stocks and whipping posts are preserved on a space below the churchyard, and the ancient village pond is nearby, but the ducking stool and posts rotted away years ago.

It is a very personal village; one family can trace their ancestors back three centuries or more – they are the Paynes of Cork's Hill and have been basket-makers and fishermen for three or more centuries.

Forthampton Cottage, a big house tenanted at the end of the last century by Mrs Sercold, had its ghost story. Two maids were in the garden one evening when a ghost rushed at them flapping big white wings and shrieking loudly. They were both terrified so the place became 'haunted' and children ran quickly past in the evenings.

It was many years afterwards the true story was told. The gardener had been missing choice strawberries, he was told that maids had been seen picking them in the late evening. He waited in a nearby shed and when he saw the maids, rushed out with the sheet flapping. As one maid fainted and the other had hysterics and the doctor had to be sent for, he was afraid to tell anyone for many years.

Frampton-on-Severn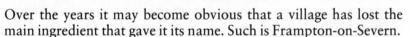

Over the years it may become obvious that a village has lost the main ingredient that gave it its name. Such is Frampton-on-Severn.

A quiet, yet thriving community, it is indeed within sight of the river Severn, but there is the rub. The river can only be reached by crossing a canal, several stiles and at least three fields. But having said that, it is worth the view when you find it. Surely a much truer picture would be brought to mind by the title Frampton-on-the-Green. A vast expanse of lush meadow grass some 700 metres long and 120 metres wide at its broadest, stretching almost the whole length of the village, it provides a delightful greeting to visitors. It is extremely well kept (tethered ponies help a great deal) and very tidy. Indeed Frampton has won the Bledisloe Cup for the largest best kept village in Gloucestershire on no less than 5 occasions.

73

Gently breaking this green landscape are three large village ponds. All have been cleared and cleaned over the last few years and have now become a haven for wildlife. The two ponds at the top of the green are the home of a pair of mute swans, Henry and Rosamunde, named after Henry II and his mistress Rosamunde Clifford who resided at Frampton Manor, a delightful Tudor manor house overlooking the pond.

The swans compete for food with a heron, moorhens, coots, many mallard, brown ducks and the Aylesbury drake from Manor Farm. Their diet is liberally supplemented by both locals and visitors who come to view the latest clutch of cygnets. The lower pond supports a colony of Great Crested Newts.

Much of Frampton's growth was due to the Cadbury's Chocolate Factory being built on the banks of the Sharpness to Gloucester canal where barges carried the rough baked chocolate from Frampton to be refined at Bournville near Birmingham.

Most of the older council houses situated at the top end of the green were built to house the Cadbury workers that came to find work at the factory after the Second World War. Sadly the factory closed several years ago and the site has been turned into an

74

Industrial Park providing a few jobs for locals but many of the newer houses have been taken by commuters to Gloucester and Bristol due to its proximity to the A38 and M5.

The Green itself supports much activity, a good class of cricket is played throughout the summer, but in August the players pull stumps and the annual Frampton Feast takes place.

It is presumed the origin of this fun-packed weekend must have been a hiring fair and livestock market but now it is a funfair and the roasting of a deer on a spit; the first slice of venison being presented to Lady of the Manor Mrs Henrietta Clifford.

Another annual event on the Green is the Elver Eating Competition. Held on Easter Monday it takes the form of several men eating 1 lb of fried baby eels known as elvers that have been caught in the Severn. The object is to see who can clear their plates in the least time to get in the *Guinness Book of Records*. Competitors have come from all over the country.

This tight-knit village continues to prosper, accepting the new, yet keeping long held tradition alive, with the green providing an enchanting backcloth.

Frocester

'Frocester? that must be Roman', said the stranger studying the signpost. How true; in two thousand acres are three known farms or villas. The Romans must have liked the place. They knew too, the importance of Frocester as a staging post for those carrying vital supplies of iron from Dean, over the Newnham–Arlingham crossing, and up the hill to cities like Cirencester and Bath.

The monks of Gloucester Abbey owned the lands until The Dissolution. Between 1284–1306 they had built 'The Great Barn of Froucester', in which to store the tithes collected in kind from the estate. Judging by the great size of the barn, sixty-two yards by ten yards, it must have been still a fertile, productive area. This tithe barn is one of the largest in the country, still in use today, and the owner of the Court is pleased to allow interested people to visit.

At the crossroads is the Royal Gloucester Hussar Hotel, first an alehouse, and then in 1759 enlarged when it became the first staging post on the Gloucester to Bath stagecoach route. It was essential to have large stables, as extra horses were necessary to negotiate the steep hill. These stables were in what is now the playing field. The alehouse was renamed the New George Inn.

A well-known character who may have been happy with Frocester was Sir Harry Lauder. He visited friends at the Court, and whilst walking in a covert, found a most distinctive contorted hazel bush, from which he cut his famous walking stick.

For centuries Frocester church, St Peter's, was a mile along the Coaley Road, and a chapel-of-ease, St Andrew's, near the crossroads. After alternate periods of decay, rebuilding and decline, St Andrew's became the parish church in 1950. A number of artifacts from St Peter's are incorporated into this immaculately kept church. The stone from St Peter's was given to Wycliffe College and used by the boys to rebuild their chapel, and only the spire and lychgate remain in their peaceful home, a quiet place of pilgrimage.

A quick check will show a hotel, eight farms and forty houses, homes for some 140 people, as compared with 400 early last century. Added to this, is Frocester Manor, since 1962 a branch of the Home Farm Trust, where 35 handicapped people of all ages live and work together in a happy, caring environment.

We have a very lively, long established cricket club which in the thirteen years of the National Village Knockout Cup has four times reached the last sixteen. Each year with Dursley Lions the Club runs a Beer Festival, again bringing many visitors and raising much money for charity.

Of characters there are plenty, but few to beat the 19th century farmer who built an elegant house for his mistress – adjoining his farm, or the squire who kept his illegitimate son on a smallholding as far from anyone as possible, but the headless lady still takes her lonely walk ready to deter any Coaley bell thieves.

This village is a place of tranquillity and beautiful views masking a hive of activity and the villagers, like the Romans, like it very much.

Guiting Power 🦢

'Gyting broc' can be traced back to AD 780 in a charter of that date and again in 974 mention is made of 'Gutinges Aeweline' –

the great spring of Guiting; later in the 13th century it became
Guiting Power, the addition being derived from the family Le Poer
who owned land in the area.

In 1958 the manor estate was bought by Mr E. R. Cochrane;
this consisted of about one thousand acres and fifty of the hundred
houses in the village. Most of these houses were placed in the
Guiting Manor Trust, a charity created for the purpose of restor-
ing and modernising the houses for letting. The work was heavily
subsidised at first, but the Trust has been self supporting since
1966. In 1977 the Guiting Amenity Trust replaced the former one
and is designed to secure the future of the village land and houses
of the local community. As a charity it pays no income tax or
inheritance tax. Four more houses were bought as they became
available and eight flatlets for elderly tenants have been built in
converted farm buildings. It was indeed fortunate for the village
when someone with such foresight and sympathy bought the
estate, insuring that the beauty and rural atmosphere would be
retained.

The village houses help to give continuity to life in Guiting
Power, but it is the people who makes its history. Not many
Cotswold villages with a population of about 300 can boast eleven
families with three generations living in the village. The Trust's
policy of choosing its tenants from local families and from people
working in or near the village and also giving priority to young
married couples, has given the population balance and stability.
Many residents have generations of forbears who lived here and
forged the sturdy independent character of the community. Life
goes on busily and steadily until some event or person rouses local
feeling, such as High Church practices in the 19th century, boast-
ful Fascist campers in the 20th, a right of way threatened or oil
prospectors drilling in the parish. Then the village vigorously
expresses its view or takes action.

The Village Hall is the centre of so many activities and the
beautiful site was given in 1961 by Mr E. R. Cochrane and makes
a wonderful setting for the eight day Festival of Music and Art, an
event held annually in July since 1971, with nightly concerts and
an exhibition of painting daily.

Guiting Power village school was opened in 1872 and now,
helped by the Trust's housing policy it has over thirty pupils. The
village feels very fortunate in still being able to retain its school,

knowing full well the deep seated sense of belonging it gives the children to start their formal education in familiar surroundings with home close by.

Dedicated to St Michael, the church was built in Norman times and has two very beautiful doorways of that period.

Towards the end of the 19th century when the boom in farming was over, the church and the rest of the village fell upon hard times and by 1902 there remained only the crumbling fabric of a once lovely church. In 1903 by wonderful efforts of the then vicar a complete restoration was carried out at a cost of £2,600.

In 1965 the Guiting Power Nature Reserve was formed around the old fish ponds on land which has now been presented by Mr E. R. Cochrane to the Gloucestershire Trust for Nature Conservation. The reserve is a good example of a wet Cotswold valley on the Upper Lias, comprising four main ecological zones: water, reed swamp, marsh, valley bank, with all plant and animal species they contain. The area covers some seventeen acres and is of particular interest in that it has suffered little recent interference by man.

Hartpury 🦢

A deadly twist in the road from Gloucester to the M50 forces the motorist to be aware of Hartpury – otherwise he might tear through this village with 'five ends and no middle' without a second glance.

'Corsend, Buttersend, Moorend, Blackwellsend and Murrelsend, five ends and no middle' says Mel Jones, born in Hartpury in the 1920s, knowing every inch of the lanes and fields as a lad – though now living in 'foreign territory' ten miles away and over the Herefordshire border into the bargain.

Down past a mixture of old and new houses, Corsend leads, after two miles of hair-raising turns to the church of St Mary the Virgin. You are advised to take these curves gently, especially at night as you skirt the village pond, or you may find yourself joining the fleet of white ducks drifting gently on the moonlit water!

Through a tunnel of ancient oak trees – perhaps survivors of the forest which once covered the area – Corsend finally brings you, past the turnings for Blackwellsend and Buttersend, onto the level land beside the church.

These two lanes, part of the complicated tracery of ancient tracks connecting outlying farmhouses and cottages, are now metalled, and, once a week, the country bus trundles round that way to pick up cottage folk from their garden gates for a jaunt into Gloucester. Where else would you find a bus driver who leaps from his seat to carry shopping bags, pushchairs and babies down the steep steps, or sits quietly gazing into the distance while those of us who have not met for a week, catch up on the local news while fumbling for our fares?

The church, built on the outer edge of the parish at the end of the 14th century after the Black Death had decimated the local population, represents, one would suppose, a hopeful new beginning. Squat and simple, with a small square tower and beautiful timber-framed porch, it stands among the green meadows with only the newly repaired tithe barn and the Court Farm for company. Hartpury Court once had its own private chapel, but this is now a tool shed and its land beside the water now supports one of the finest Jersey herds in the country.

A little further on is the Leadon river, narrow, and unassuming but deeply dangerous and with spiteful habits, rapidly engulfing the meadows after a summer storm, obliterating the little flat bridge and causing the quick withdrawal of cattle from the level pasture lands. And many a local boy has had cause to thank the

Leadon for a day off school in the days when the bus taking them that way to the secondary school at Newent would be stopped in its tracks by suddenly rising water.

A short distance from the bridge is Hartpury Mill, its great wooden wheel still in place, its glassy millpond draped in weeping willows. A place for artists and photographers to sign over!

Down Murrelsend, past yet another string of pretty cottages you come to Hartpury Farm Institute where young people in green wellies run the farm with a neat perfection not seen in the muddled barnyards of old Gloucestershire. The main building, once a dignified gentlemen's residence with its attractive lawns and walled kitchen garden now houses the offices and classrooms of this busy College of Agriculture.

Moorend will bring you back to the Gloucester road past a jumble of little dwellings built for the servants of Hartpury House, now modernised and variously occupied by staff of the college.

On the other side of the main road the land rises steeply to a ridge overlooking the Vale of Severn. Nestling by the roadside, backed by trees is the village school, a small stone building, now bursting at the seams and sprouting terrapin classrooms in its ample playground.

Further along the road the narrow Hiam's Lane runs up through the woods to the Rising Sun, a pub aptly named as it stands on top of the hill looking out over the Severn valley towards the distant line of the Cotswolds on the eastern side. But why, may one ask, do all the locals call this pub The Salt Box? No-one seems able to answer that!

Two more 'pubs' grace the main road through the village. Near the Ashleworth turn, the Royal Exchange, its ordinary looks belying its grandiose name, woos the passer-by with a burst of fairy lights and offers of good food, while further along the road is the old Canning Arms named for the former owners of Hartpury House. Stories are still told of a landlord of the 'Cannon' as it is called, who ruled his customers with a rod of iron, banging the bar with his fist if they got too noisy, and on no account allowing any singing! Yet people from far and near flocked into the 'Cannon' to sit on uncomfortable benches at the bare, scrubbed tables while smarter places nearby were left half empty!

Hawling 🌿

Follow Tally Ho Lane out of Guiting Power and it will lead you into the village of Hawling, one of many villages in the Cotswold Hills which are so small as to be more properly called hamlets. Most of these lie in the folds of the hills but Hawling is an exception situated as it is, some 900 feet above sea level. A true hill village that has a regular period of solitude each year when snow invades and leaves the inhabitants to their own devices. Rudders *A New History of Gloucestershire* describes it as 'remarkable for its healthy air, sound sheep and sweet mutton' – this still follows today, as any farmer there will vouch.

Hawling can boast of neither shops, post office or even a pub. Some thirty houses, a church, chapel and small village hall is the extent of the existing village – 'no frills' as the villagers say.

It does not seem long ago that Mr Edgeworth, the postman, who lived at Andoversford, brought letters and parcels from there, walking to Syreford, Sevenhampton, Brockhampton, Hawling, Shewell Hill, Hawling Lodge and Tally Ho. There, in return for a meal, he would do about two hours gardening and walk back to Andoversford, blowing a whistle at each place to give warning that he was there to carry letters etc. back to the post office. He did that journey for thirty nine years in all winds and weather.

Many of the women worked in the fields and, like the men, had to be sure of waterproof footwear. Boots could be made to measure by Oliver Wood. His boots were completely waterproof and would last for several years. Oliver was born, lived his life and died in the same house in Sevenhampton. His boots were a byword for miles around and if a man was seen to be limping he was advised to get Oliver 'to stretch em' or 'rub the badgers' fat in a bit harder'.

If the doctor was needed, a member of the family would walk some six miles to Winchcombe to the surgery and the doctor would make his way to the village on horseback. A midwife lived in the village; she also did the work of a nurse and was a help and friend to all.

Having no shop, the housewife had to think well ahead in order to cater for her family. The groceries were delivered once a month, a butcher called once a week and the baker twice.

Mr Harwood the baker, came from Salperton and always wore a flour covered bowler hat and his long whiskers were dyed brown from his old clay pipe. But he made 'the fairest dough cakes' ever tasted. If the snow lay too deep for him to reach the village, two men would set out on foot with a long bath and collect enough bread from the bake house to supply the families of Hawling.

If you wanted to visit Cheltenham you had a choice of transport: shank's pony to Notgrove Station (three miles) or by the carriers cart. Mr Mile's cart was not too comfortable. There were no windows to look out and only bare hard seats along the side of the van. The middle of the van was loaded with a variety of parcels, eggs, sacks of corn, rabbits and anything else the carrier was asked to take. The journey took about two hours each way and on the return anyone who could walk was expected to do so when there was a hill to climb.

Small and quiet sums up Hawling, but how nice that the inhabitants know each other by their Christian names.

Highnam 🪶

Highnam lies about two miles from Gloucester between the roads to Ross and Newent, including the hamlets of Over and Linton, with Lassington.

The Manor House dates back before 1080 when it was the property of the Abbey of St Peter, now Gloucester Cathedral.

The Manor remained in possession of the Abbey until the Dissolution by Henry VIII, when it passed down through many notable families. In 1837, with 1100 acres, a wharf at Over, mill and woodlands, it was purchased by Thomas Hubert Parry, a wealthy, cultured gentleman and well-known painter of frescoes, in a style perfected by him. A collector of art, paintings and glass, he travelled with his wife adding to his treasures, altering and extending the house, creating the gardens, engaging the services of James Pulham, a leading exponent of rockwork, whose work in these gardens is the largest and finest in the country; planting rare specimens of trees and plants he had collected, draining the boglands, turning them into lakes and fishponds.

His wife Isabella suggested the idea that a church would be of benefit to scattered residents of the village. She bore several children, some of whom died in infancy. After her death, Parry embarked upon the project to build the church as a memorial to her and to the children they had lost, naming it The Church of the Holy Innocents. Being well set back from the road, surrounded by fields and trees, it is a delightful church to visit, with its frescoes and wall paintings almost as fresh as when Parry painted them, its slender spire, a copy of the spire of Salisbury Cathedral, a landmark for many miles around.

Parry also built many cottages of various designs to house the tenants of the growing parish, encouraging them to further their skills. The first two at Popes Pool were occupied by a tailor and a maker of straw hats. In the same stone as that of the church, he also built a parsonage, school, schoolhouse and lodge for the sacristan, all in an idyllic setting overlooking the 'Lime Walk', a large green, now the cricket field; also the newly planted Pinetum, where flourished wild birds, rare trees and flowers of much interest to the Royal Horticultural Society.

The Women's Institute was formed in 1920 by Mrs Gambier Parry. Membership though small, became an important introduction to village life, bringing together the few women who could attend. It played an important part too during the war years by making, on primus stoves, thousands of pounds of jam, bottling and canning countless pounds of fruit. Electricity had not been connected, coal was severely rationed, each member sparing one lump to start the wood boiler, then scouring the parkland for wood to keep it boiling for canning. Water too was not connected but carried from school to Council House, as the Village Hall was then known; later one tap was installed, but not a kitchen. With lungs and eyes full of wood smoke, weary arms and legs, the work was carried on under great difficulties, but tremendous team spirit. Life was made much easier when, after many months, this was transferred to the comfort and convenience of the dairy at Linton Farm. In addition, members held many other fund-raising efforts – whist-drives in their homes, sharing precious rations for refreshments, knitting balaclavas, socks, etc., also auctions to assist the Red Cross organisation. The Diamond Jubilee of the Movement was celebrated in great style in 1980, membership being about 45 and with recent housing development in the area it is still growing. Of course, it must not be overlooked that members are particularly proud to live in the village in which the famous composer Parry was born, who composed the stirring music to William Blake's poem, *Jerusalem*, which is sung at every meeting, the length and breadth of the country.

Horsley 🌿

Horsley is almost a hidden village, with most of the houses nestling in steep valleys either side of the main street. It was in existence at the time of the Domesday Book, when it belonged to Norman monks.

A priory was built, which, in 1732, came into the possession of the English Abbey of Bruton. This fell into disrepair in the 15th century due to the Prior of that time spending the revenues on travel and good living.

A prison was then built on the site and was, for 100 years, one of the four county prisons of Gloucestershire.

At about the same time, Horsley Court was built. This was originally a Tudor cottage which was greatly enlarged in 1700 and became a magistrates court. In the large room which is now a dining room, part of the ceiling could be raised, leaving a lattice-work grill through which members of the public could watch the court proceedings. Justice must have been thirsty work as there are still large cider barns behind the Court and a huge stone wheel and trough for crushing the apples, complete with a wooden yoke for a horse, is still there. There is an unusual dovecote at the Court, built about 1690, which was probably originally a granary store. The roof has oval holes in it, known as 'owl holes' which served as ventilation holes and also encouraged owls to catch mice and so prevent them from eating the grain. A huge cedar tree stood in the grounds from which Judge Jeffreys was supposed to hang offenders.

It is quite likely that Judge Jeffreys visited Horsley, but the unfortunate offenders were more likely to have been hanged outside the prison walls. Until quite recently there was an underground passage running from the Priory to the ground just outside the east wall of the prison. Here the last people to be hanged for sheep-stealing in Gloucestershire are reputed to have met their end.

The prison was closed following the Prison Reform Act and

rebuilt as a private house, which was once more known as the Priory. Today it is the property of Gloucestershire County Council.

The church, which was rebuilt in about 1840, was originally built about 1300 and today only the tower remains of the original church. It does boast one small claim to fame. In 1732, the vicar of that time performed a 'Half Marriage'. The church records for August 11th, 1732 read, 'John Pegler and Ann Thomas were half married August 11th. I proceeded no further because they paid me but one half 2s.6d'. Speculation as to which half was married and how legal it was continue to this day!

Horsley has never been a really important place, nor has it ever been a particularly rich place. But, for over 900 years people have lived in this pleasant part of a beautiful county. Today people have more time to appreciate their surroundings and there is still a strong community spirit among the present day dwellers in Horsley.

Hucclecote 🌿

One day, in the 1950s, old Hucclecote finally had to admit to the arrival of the 20th century when the 'Top Shop' was demolished. For as long as we could remember the little general shop at the corner of Churchdown Lane had supplied all our needs. Granted, the customers stood in serried ranks, hoping their turn would come soon, while the gossip and repartee flew to and fro, but did they have to build a serve-yourself-mini-market with strip lighting and totally annihilate the old place? For, when the dust had settled, or so it seemed, there was nothing but an asphalt car park and not a sign to show where it had been.

Well, that's not the only piece of Hucclecote history to have gone underground long ago but one, at least, will remain. Straight as an arrow from Gloucester, through Hucclecote and Brockworth and on up the Cotswold scarp to Cirencester runs Ermin Street, one of the many Roman roads which have helped to shape the face of England, and Hucclecote, like many other villages has blossomed along this trunk.

Half a mile away from the road, down Green Lane was the old village green, a few houses, a couple of farms, a duck pond, orchards and quiet fields. Now the M5 cuts a swathe through the farm land and the farmer's cattle were greatly surprised to find themselves crossing a great-arched bridge from one field to another.

Until the mid-19th century there was no church at Hucclecote and the people from around here went along Churchdown Lane to the ancient church on top of Chosen Hill a couple of miles away to the north. Along this lane is 'The Nook' where peacocks roosting in the trees would set up a screaming at passers by.

Some of the inhabitants of the new estates along the Hucclecote Road would be surprised at what lies under their feet. Do the people of one new road know, for instance, that they are living in Fred Matthew's coal yard? And what of the neat houses of another Hucclecote estate which was once the nursery of a well known rose grower? George, who worked at the nursery as a young man, remembers a well, covered by a huge stone in the gardens there. Many of these wells were beautifully made, walled in stone to quite a depth and widening out at the bottom like a bottle. 'You could turn a horse and cart down there' he says with some exaggeration!

A hundred years ago Hucclecote was the place to live if you were newly rich, and many business men from Gloucester had handsome houses with large gardens here – now, too large for the modern family, they are turning into retirement homes, flats or private nursing homes or being demolished to make room for new development. A great outcry was heard recently when a massive cedar tree in the grounds of one large house was felled to make room for flats.

Poor old Hucclecote! It is slowly melting into the arms of the City of Gloucester. Even the old Wagon and Horses where, in the early part of the century, race horses were stabled and exercised in the paddocks behind, has a sparkling new look about it now and boasts a skittle alley where the stabling used to be.

Huntley 🦚

Huntley is situated about half-way between Gloucester and Ross-on-Wye, at the edge of the Forest of Dean. A century ago the village was split into two areas, with some cottages and a few shops near the Red Lion and in North Road; and about twenty cottages on Huntley Hill in Smokey Bottom and Deep Filling, plus several scattered Estate Farms.

Benjamin St John Ackers bought Huntley Manor House and estate which consisted of 1133 acres in 1884 and came to live here on the slopes of Mayhill with his family. A well-educated man, he had many and varied interests in life. Likewise his son, Major Charles Penryn Ackers, whose love of trees resulted in him becoming one of the leading authorities on forestry in this country.

After the First World War he started expanding farming and forestry in all directions – creating work for the men of the village.

At a peak time 220 men were employed. Now much is sold and only Woodland Improvement Ltd. continue to grow young forest trees. The Estate Woodlands and farmlands have diminished considerably employing very few people.

St John The Baptist Church was rebuilt on the site of a 12th century church in 1861 at the expense of Rev. Daniel Capper, a wealthy man who also financed the building of the Manor House in the French Chateau style.

Huntley Court – at one time the main house of the village dates back to being an old coaching inn known as The White Heart possibly until about 1700. In 1768 records show that Edmund Probyn, biggest landowner in the area of Newland to Newent, owned it – since when it has changed hands many times. Early this century garden parties were held on its spacious lawns, and later village fetes.

The old Tithe Barn nearby is a fine example of Tudor times. The original Queen beams and three wattle and daub panels are still in good condition. Over four hundred years ago a garrison of Cromwellian soldiers sheltered here waiting to go into battle.

Like most village businesses the local grocery and bakery was a family concern. The Green brothers continued in the mould set by their father, for changes came slowly to the country villages. Although small, the shop sold literally everything, from grocery to greengrocery, animal food-stuffs, ironmongery, hardware, and haberdashery.

The bakehouse was situated at the back of the shop, and the bakers started work at eleven o'clock at night to mix and knead the dough, which was heavy work done by hand. The hot ovens made working conditions very warm and exhausting for the men,

who were liable to easily catch cold when they went out into the chill night air to their homes to snatch a few hours sleep. They returned early in the morning to find the dough risen and ready to be shaped into loaves and baked in the large stone ovens.

Charlie Green with the help of Percy delivered goods to the neighbouring villages within a four mile radius of the shop. There were oil cans to be filled, corn and meal to be weighed into bags, as well as groceries, bread and cakes to load, so that it was lunchtime before they were ready to set off.

Shopping day was looked forward to by many as a break from the routine of the week, and a chance of having a gossip with any acquaintances one might meet in the village. Mr Cooper, the local postman, was quite a character and loved nothing better than to throw his bag down in the shop and talk and joke with the staff and pull their legs; but if his wife came in he turned as meek as a mouse!

Kemble 🍃

A river that only sometimes flows; the lone skeleton of a rich Roman lady; a station without platform tickets next to a tunnel that's not a tunnel at all, and the 'red light' district of the church: these are the enigmas that are Kemble.

Kemble is the first village along the course of the Thames. The earliest records are of a Saxon settlement, established after the Battle of Dyrham in AD 577. The Romans were, of course, in the area before then, but evidence of their presence in Kemble remained obscure. No-one thought of Kemble as being a Roman settlement; not, that is, until 8th March 1983, when John Gillet, while converting a stable in West Lane uncovered a Roman coffin dated between AD 100 and AD 400, containing the bones of a middle-aged Roman lady. It is now in the Corinium Museum.

The observant visitor will find another mystery nearby. Off the A429, Station Road crosses the railway line. Look eastwards from the bridge to the mouth of Kemble tunnel. Look again. No natural hillock surmounts the opening; the 'tunnel' is a 415-yard stretch of line roofed in between the embankments! This operation was executed on the insistence of Robert Gordon, MP, who employed most of the villagers on his farm estate, and whose land the Swindon/Cheltenham line crossed when it opened in May 1841. Not content with handsome compensation, he demanded that neither noisy train nor dirty smoke should spoil the view from his newly-renovated Kemble House, hence the artificial tunnel. Squire Robert never allowed a station on his land. Passengers connecting for Cirencester had only a draughty wooden shed for shelter. No Kemble Junction was mentioned in those early printed time-tables. The only people who joined or left the Cheltenham and Great Western Union at Kemble were members of the Gordon family, who had a private pathway to the 'station'. The public had to walk a mile to Tetbury Road, just outside Gordon territory.

When the present station was built in 1872 it became a focal point in the village, employing many besides the occupants of the twelve Railway Cottages. Hitching rings, used for horse-drawn milk and mail wagons, can still be seen in the cut lime-stone station wall. Horses from Cirencester were stabled overnight. After taking London-bound evening mail to Kemble they awaited the 4.30 a.m. mail and newspaper train the next day. The clanging of milk-churns, the swish of water as Royal trains for South Wales filled up from Kemble water tower (which also supplied the whole of Swindon railway works as well as stand-pipes in the village) were everyday sounds at the turn of the century.

Even since the 1963 Beeching axe cut the branch line to Cirencester, the station has been well-used and the car parks full. No platform ticket is required at Kemble, for the public has a right-of-way to the post-box beyond the booking office. But alas there is no refreshment room. Passengers must rely for a cup of tea on the award-winning goodwill of the cheery station staff, for in 1872 Miss Anna, Squire Gordon's daughter, insisted that no refreshments be allowed. This would have meant the sinful sale of alcohol. The coffee tavern was, however, tolerated. Successive proprietors like Josiah Winchcombe, who was there in 1900, were no doubt grateful for the chance of a living, but, wishing for a better living from the sale of alcohol, probably cursed the Gordon family for their strict principles!

Michael Biddulph, who inherited the Estate from the childless Miss Anna, continued the ban, and it was not until 1948 when Kemble Estate was bought by Cornishman Samuel Phillips, that the first licence was approved for 'The Tavern'. Foreign students at Kemble's Western Language Centre might well appreciate this slice of old England, where the local skittles team plays, and the well-tended gardens, the hanging baskets and the late Victorian ironwork which grace Kemble Station.

Kempley ༄

In 1086 Kempley had ten villagers, seven smallholders with twelve ploughs and seven slaves. Its value was £5 and its acreage 1800. In the 12th century a small church, St Mary's was built, possibly on the bridle path between Hereford and Gloucester. It contains the most astonishing frescoes, of St Peter and the apostles, of 'Our Lord in Majesty' with his feet resting on a globe, and of the de Lacy family to whom William the Conqueror gave Kempley. These frescoes were hidden for hundreds of years – probably white-washed over by Puritans – and only rediscovered in 1872. They were covered with a coat of varnish which it was hoped would

protect them, but it darkened and once again the paintings were hidden. In 1955 Mrs Baker of the Royal College of Art began to remove the coat of varnish and found the frescoes in good condition. Under the care of the Department of the Environment restoration work is continuing.

The village gradually began to move uphill to avoid floods and fog, the old church became dilapidated and in 1903 St Edward's was built under the patronage of the Earl Beauchamp. It has an unusual latticed window known locally as the Jam Tart window. The stones came from the Forest of Dean, timber from the woods, and local craftsmen helped build it. The iron work and nails were made by George Smallman the blacksmith, Edward Barnsley made the lectern and Ernest Gimson the candlesticks. Local people painted the figures of Mary and John on the gable beam. The church was admired by John Betjeman on one of his ecclesiastical explorations.

Both churchyards are a glorious sight in spring when wild daffodils carpet the grass and fill the local woods. Daffodil teas are an annual institution in the parish hall and raise money for the church. One Sunday near Easter is designated 'Daffodil Sunday'

and there are walks led by the Chief Forester and local conservation groups. Villagers are divided about the influx of outsiders —
needed to raise money but sometimes destructive although the
wild flowers are protected by law. Fifty years ago nearly all the
fields were full of wild daffodils and picking did little harm but
modern farming methods have reduced them; only two fields in
Kempley show how they used to grow, but they still line the edges
of fields and road verges.

Farming in the area is mixed — dairy, sheep and arable on the
heavy clay soil. There are plenty of orchards, including trees of
cider apple and perry pear. The village has always been famous for
its cider although this is now made just outside its boundaries. It
was said that Kempley folk were long lived because of their cider
drinking. One vicar, the Rev. Peter Senhouse was in office for 67
years and Rudder's 1779 history states that one household of
sixteen persons had not known a death in living memory!

In spite of its cider-making tradition there is no pub in Kempley
and the only organisation is the W.I. A mile and a half from a main
road, Kempley retains its village atmosphere and with its trades
and activities it is a living community.

Kilcot & Gorsley 🌿

Kilcot and Gorsley are two small villages on the borders of
Gloucestershire and Herefordshire. They are joined by a busy and
sometimes dangerous main road used by traffic to reach the M50
Ross Spur. The villages are divided by the county boundary, which
leaves half of Gorsley in Herefordshire and half with Kilcot in
Gloucestershire. This means that one group of children go to
Gorsley and Ross-on-Wye schools and the others to Newent
schools. It has a strange effect on shopping habits too, as one end
of the village travels to Ross and Hereford and the other to
Newent and Gloucester, so that the two districts are quite separate.

The district is suitable for market gardening, the vegetables and
fruit being transported to South Wales and Cheltenham market.
There is a modern fruit farm and orchards of cherry, cider apple
and pear trees, making the village well worth a visit in blossom
time.

Neither village has a real centre, though both have pubs and post office stores. Kilcot boasts a small common, which was used for cricket games and its pond for sliding on in winter and tadpole catching in spring. All that, alas, has long since gone; it's used now for a council stone tip and all its paths are lost under the scrub. No longer do you see gypsy caravans parked on the common over-night with piebald horses hobbled nearby. There was a spring of drinking water on the lower common and this made a convenient stopping place for them on the way to Wales.

Much of Kilcot land was given to the Hooke family in the Elizabethan era for some valiant deed and descendants are still in the village, though not the Lord of the Manor – he lives in London. Originally, Conigree Court was his family's residence, just one of the fairly large houses in Kilcot, the Hooke's Briary Hill House being another. Many large old farm houses remain, but Bob Powell's smithy has disappeared and you can no longer get your accumulator charged at Percy James's or buy sweets at Mrs Buckland's shop, half-way down Kilcot Hill. Nor can you spend all day sampling home made cider at the local farms. Cider was made at three or four mills in Kilcot, the horse plodding round and round the mill, while the stone crushed the apples and anything else in the trough. There followed days of tasting the different vintages, resulting in loud singing and even baying at the moon during the nights.

Our village has had its share of famous people and boasts one house with a light blue plaque. This records the fact that Rutland Boughton, the composer, lived in Kilcot. At one time, his *Immortal Hour* was highly praised and will probably return to popularity. His house became the meeting place for famous singers, including Paul Robeson, and the refuge during the war for Ludvic Koch, the pioneer of Natural History recordings. Once, the impressive Linton Hall, standing in the middle of Gorsley, not Linton, was a pub, but later housed Hildagard and Hildabrand Mosley, the sisters of the famous Sir Oswald.

War time in Kilcot started off with evacuees from Birmingham, but they came during the 'phoney war' of 1939 and had all returned home long before the bombing started. The children were an eye-opener for the local children, they even took tap-dancing lessons!

One memorable night, a bomb dropped on Kilcot. I suppose one of the planes that droned over continuously must have found it had one bomb left in its bay and decided to get rid of it. The whole village seems to have heard it whooshing down, everyone tried to struggle under beds – not easy when you are in a panic. However, the bomb fell at an angle into a bank of lawn at Mrs Cook's and did very little damage – just some broken glass in the conservatory. We all met to view the big hole next day.

Today, most of us find the villages lovely places to live in, with plenty of interesting things to do and the town easy to reach if you have a car.

Kingscote 🦢

In 19th century Kingscote, sport must have featured largely for many in the community, whether taking part in it or in a back-up capacity.

In the early 1800s Robert Kingscote laid out a fine race-course in the grounds of his new Georgian-style mansion, which became known as the Goodwood of the West, and a secluded dell in the park was the scene of many prize-fights.

Cricket, too, flourished for a time at Kingscote. Henry Kingscote was president of the Marylebone Cricket Club at the age of 25 in 1827. *Scores and Biographies* said this of him:

> Mr Kingscote comes next, as fine a young man
> As ever was built upon nature's best plan;
> He stands six feet four – and, what don't often follow,
> His leg is a model to form an Apollo.
>
> A fine slashing hitter as ever was found
> He sometimes has knocked the ball out of the ground;
> An excellent thrower, a hundred yards clear,
> And ladies protest that he runs like a deer.

There was the celebrated occasion at Lord's where in a two-day match in 1871 (sic) the MCC were beaten by over 250 runs by the Kingscote Club, augmented by James Broadbridge of Sussex, at one time the best 'general cricketer' in England whose round-armed bowling in 1827 effected a revolution in the cricketing world; James Saunders, a butcher from Haselmere, Surrey, who kept wicket; and John Bayley, a Mitcham tailor who had been first engaged as a cricketer by the Kingscote Club but in 1823 had become a practice bowler at Lord's, continuing as 'a faithful servant' until 1854 when he was 60 years of age.

For a time towards the end of the century coursing flourished in Kingscote. And of course with the hounds by then kennelled at Uley, 3 miles down the road, foxhunting was always a popular pursuit whether mounted or as a follower on foot. The shoot supported a couple of gamekeepers, their dogs, and a pheasantry which was almost in the village.

Kingswood 🦌

Kingswood's claim to fame resides in the past, rather than the present, when it was the site of a large Cistercian Abbey, alas destroyed by Henry VIII's minions. All that remains is one gatehouse. Some of the stones were used to build Newark Park, and it is said the Abbot can sometimes be seen there, wandering round trying to reclaim his property.

People used to come from all over Europe for the miraculous cures alleged to take place here and to buy indulgences granted by the Pope. Sceptics will point out the Abbey was short of money at the time because most of the lay brothers and half of the villagers had been wiped out by the Black Death. For centuries nobody would put a spade into the corner of the graveyard where tradition says the victims are buried.

The Lay Chapel remained as the Parish Church until it was replaced in 1723 by the present building.

The monks, who were responsible for the setting up of the clothing industry over a wide area, left a legacy of mills right through the Little Avon valley. Though no longer producing cloth, work is still being done on four of these sites in the parish. The Little Avon, once used for water power, still meanders through the lower part of the village and is home to a large family of ducks that squabble over the bread thrown to them by yet another generation of children.

Country people being well-known for their independent views, it is not surprising that there has been a flourishing fellowship of

Dissenters – now known as Congregationalists – in the village since the early 1600s. Both standing on the Abbey precincts the Church and Chapel have lived side by side through conflict and harmony for over three centuries.

The oldest village tradition, the pulling of the curfew bell at 8 p.m. each evening, ceased when the ringing of bells was made the alarm signal for Hitler's expected invasion. Many older residents can recall that, when children, the curfew's call summoned them home to bed on a summer's evening, no excuses being accepted as the bell could be heard all over the parish, even by the boys swimming in the chilly waters of the Pound upstream at Nind Mill.

Present day 'pilgrims' come from all round the neighbourhood to use the fine Village Hall. While not offering cures, it provides facilities for all sorts of pastimes from discos to W.I., boxing to Brownies.

Being only 1¼ miles away Kingswood lives in the shadow of Wotton-under-Edge, making use of the facilities while keeping its own identity. It makes no claim to be a beauty spot or an exclusive address, but in keeping with the traditions of the English country-side it is a very friendly place to live.

Lechlade 🌿

Lechlade is a pleasant place situated on the river Thames, where it is joined by the Leach (from which it takes its name). It grew in importance on receiving a Worlut Charter early in the 13th century. This became well known for the sale of locally-made sage cheese which was produced in large quantities along the rich Thames-side meadows, some of which have delightful names. 'Butterhorns' and 'Grass-wells' speak for themselves. This cheese together with other goods was taken by barge to be sold in London thus making Lechlade a prosperous centre of commerce and transport.

The last street market was held in 1928. Let into walls are rings used in tethering horses, a horse-fair was held around September 9th each year. After harvest, races were run in Town Meadow, part of Leaze farm.

The ancient method of strip farming was in evidence in North Meadow. A plot known as 'Draw Acre' was let by ballot to tenants

96

of the meadow. Some of the stone markers may still be found. Unfortunately modern farming methods have destroyed the fritillary which grew in profusion in North Meadow. However, a few may still be found in the water meadows.

Today many residents earn their living working at the air bases of Fairford and Brize Norton and the rapidly growing town of Swindon, the river being left to pleasure craft and fishermen.

Leckhampton 🦩

The village comes under the Cheltenham hundred – first recorded as Lechentone and listed in the Domesday Book. By 1691 it had become Leckington, meaning 'Homestead', where garlic and leeks were grown. Leckhampton, now, is partly in Cheltenham Borough and partly in Tewkesbury Borough.

The present church was built on what was the site of a Saxon church – there are still remains of Norman work, but it has been much altered. The tower is 14th century, with a broach spire. The earliest recorded mention of a parish priest was 1162. The church contains some fine effigies of Sir John and Lady Gifford. In the churchyard is a large granite cross in memory of Edward Wilson who went with Scott to the South Pole and had lived at the Crippetts for some years.

Sir John Gifford was Lord of the Manor from 1300–1330 and built the earliest sections of the Court. The Giffords were descended from a famous Norman nobleman, who accompanied William the Conqueror to England was was rewarded with twenty manors – four in Gloucestershire. It is assumed that he came to Leckhampton. Through marriage the Court passed to the Norwood family in 1486. Colonel Henry, born in 1614 was a Royalist and supporter of Charles I. He was exiled and helped to establish the Colony of Virginia. He returned to England and was again involved in Royalist activities and spent the last years of his life in the Tower. In 1797 the Estate passed to the Trye family and in the early 1900s it was bought by John Hargreaves, grandson of the Hargreaves who invented the 'Spinning Jenny'. It was during that time that the Prince of Wales, accompanied by Lillie Langtry was a visitor and for their benefit the north wing was rebuilt. During the 1914–1918 War the Court was used as a V.A.D. Hospital, and in the Second World War as a prison camp. In 1957 it became a school, but is now a Cancer Care Hospice run by the Sue Ryder Foundation.

The oldest surviving cottage is Moat Cottage, together with Olde England. Moat Cottage deeds date from the 16th century – it is a 'cruck' cottage. There are six examples of wattle and daub cottages in the village. 'Cromwell Cottage' has been demolished; Cromwell is thought to have stayed there during the siege of Gloucester.

Iron Age forts are found on most of the prominent hills in the area, including Leckhampton. The stone from the quarries was used to build Cheltenham, e.g. Cheltenham College.

Charles Brandon Tyre, a surgeon and friend of Dr Jenner, owned the quarry. He was instrumental in installing a tram-way from the quarry to the main line station, thus creating the first known railway in Gloucestershire. The incline led to the formation of the 'Devil's Chimney', where quarrymen left the inferior stone which gradually developed into this landmark.

Tower Lodge on the Birdlip Road was once the 'Old Ale House' for the quarrymen. In 1938 the Lodge was the scene of the Torso Murder of Captain Butt. The torso was thrown into the Severn at Haw Bridge – the limbs were found in a nearby garden, but the head was never found. In earlier times there were allotments on the northern slopes and paths crossed in every direction. They were used by farmers and shoppers from Cowley and Cubberley. On Good Friday all the town of Cheltenham seemed to meet there. When a certain Mr Dale came into ownership of the Hill, he refused to give rights of way and built Tramway Cottage across one of the paths. After many disputes the public rebelled. In 1903 the Cottage was set alight and rioting occurred. Eight men were sent to prison. The Cottage was rebuilt and still stands. Today the Hill is under the care of the Cheltenham Council and is an enjoyable place for walking and recreation.

Littledean 🦢

The story of Littledean covers a long period, going back to prehistoric times when people called Silures inhabited this part of Gloucestershire.

We gather from Domesday that most of the Severn-Wye peninsula was split between three Saxon Thanes as caretakers for the King. In Norman times the Manor of Dene was divided and Dean Parva or Littledean came into being. Indeed, The Red House, situated at the bottom of Littledean Hill is reputed to have been built not long after the Norman invasion, possibly a guard tower or keep.

Once known as 'a jewel in a perfect setting', Littledean Grange, probably built by Sir William Kingston who was so very prominent in the execution of Anne Boleyn, was razed to the ground a few years ago. Now there are only memories and tales of ghostly ventures.

Dean Croft, an attractive red-roofed, whitewalled house thought to be early 17th century, has two interesting circular staircases built into the thickness of its walls, one of which has single blocks of solid oak for steps. The three inch thick oak top of the dining room sideboard is said to be a candle-makers bench. The windows have Tudor style drip stones and a William III penny was found in the attic.

Because of the recent discovery of a Roman Temple, Dean Hall is now a tourist attraction. Once the Manor, with the symbolic balls on the pillars of the gates, it was in 1556 the house of the High Sheriff of Gloucester, one Richard Brayne. On May 7th 1664, Parliamentary troops overcame the Royalists in Littledean. Lieutenant Colonel Congrave and Captain Wigmore had accepted quarter when a stray shot killed a trooper. Quarter forgotten, all Royalists perished, including the two officers who died in the Hall itself. A black boy who killed his master in a quarrel haunts the place and a ghostly figure, besom in hand, sweeps the leaves in the drive.

There are only photographs of the one-time cross, its name place now a small traffic roundabout. A grey lady is the ghost of 17th century Church Farm and The Old Vic, 13th century, once an Inn also boasts an apparition.

Littledean Church, mostly 14th century, has stonework in the chancel arch of Saxon origin, indicating an earlier church. It was dedicated to St Ethelbert, who was murdered by Offa his father-in-law, in the 8th century and over whose body Hereford Cathedral was built. A document dated 1477 granted the inhabitants of Littledean full control of the 'Chapel' churchyard enclosure and all its possessions, provided they undertook to pay 53s.4d annually. They could choose their own chaplain if they did not fall in arrears. Now carefully preserved under glass, the church possesses a priceless piece of 15th century needlework: once part of a priest's vestment, but altered after the Reformation and used as a funeral pall. The church bells were cast in Chepstow in 1752 and are all individually inscribed. The church school opposite was built in 1871.

Dominating this end of the village is the Forest jail or House of Correction: built as one of few in the county as a result of the work of the great prison reformer, Sir George Onesipherous Paul. The high walls conceal the inner buildings, from which only two persons ever escaped – one broke his leg falling from the wall and was recaptured in a nearby pig-sty; the other crossed the river Severn and was captured in Stroud. Sentenced for indecent assault and 'uncomparable filthery' one prisoner was made to wear a dress in the hope that he would mend his ways. A keeper, matron, parson and teacher staffed the building and inmates had day and night cells and were allowed a leg of lamb and fair allocations of bread weekly. A treadmill tells of less lenient punishment.

Mining at pits with the splendid names like Eastern United, Fancy, Cannop, Lightmoor and True Blue used to be the work of most village men, but since closure of the pits they work in local factories or commute to Gloucester.

Longhope ✿

There has been a settlement here for many centuries. The Manor of Hope is mentioned in the Domesday Book (in Westbury Hundred) when it had four ox-drawn ploughs.

Harts Barn (now a listed building and home of a farmer) was built by descendants of John the Sergeant, who was granted lands at Hope by William the Conqueror, on condition that he provided hounds when the King came to hunt hart in Dean Forest. The Manor House was converted into a hotel and more recently into a retirement home.

All Saints Church dates back to the 12th century but has been extensively restored. The arms of William III are over the door and beneath the chancel lie members of the Probyn family, Lords of the Manor.

Near the church entrance stands an old domestic mortar, used as a font from 1660 to 1860.

The present population is about 1,450. Family names mentioned in a parish record of 1608 (when there were 87 grown men) still persist – Dobbs, Read(e), Brown, Wintle, Lane and Bullock.

Estate development in the last decade brought new life to the village and especially to the schools. At a time when many villages bemoan the loss of their primary schools, Longhope has two. Longhope C. of E. (1829) is unique in that it was built within the rectory grounds, the canteen being a converted stable. Hopes Hill C.P. is attached to the Baptist Church. The Rectory is now a home for the elderly.

The village has several houses of historical interest. Royal Spring, once an inn, was so named after Charles I called in 1642 after the Battle of Powick Bridge, near Worcester, to drink from the spring or perhaps sample the local wine, as the valley was rich in vines and much wine was made. Court Leet, opposite the church, was once the local court and the adjacent cottage was the gaol. There are other half-timbered houses, some with wattle and daub walls. Knapp House can trace an indenture dated 1725 stamped with the official seal of the Duke of Kent recording its sale.

The village inns are remembered in an old saying: 'The Farmer's Boy went to The Cross to borrow The Nag to draw The Plough to The Yew Tree'. Three of these remain today.

Most notable among its village characters was Jimmy Flash, a wanderer. Local residents can remember him organising a collection round the village for his dead wife – who came back a week later! His most famous exploit was the burial of a horse, which died on the top of the hill while working. Jimmy dug a hole, rolled the horse into it and covered it, leaving its legs stuck up in the air. Word got round and village children hurried to see the sight. The farmer ordered him to do the job properly but the animal's legs by now were stiff so Jimmy took an axe and chopped them off.

The village industries of wood turning and fencing manufacture have declined but new industries have come including diamond tools, garden ornaments and clock-making.

Lydbrook 🦋

The river at Lydbrook attracts many people for coarse fishing and canoeing. The bank on the near side is a small park, with trees, flowering shrubs, flowers and seats, and this is a very popular place with visitors, especially in the summer months. On the opposite side of the river is Courtfield House, owned for many years by the Vaughan family. It is now leased to the Millhill Fathers, and used to train young men for mission work overseas.

Lydbrook was formerly a coal-mining village. The Arthur and Edward colliery, known to the locals as 'Waterloo' was situated at the upper end and people were known to put their clocks right by the pit hooter which was clearly heard by all the local inhabitants at the end of each shift. The site is now a timber yard. There was also a tinplate works and the majority of local people worked at either one of these places. Sadly they are no longer in existence, and were closed many years ago, resulting in people seeking other employment and travelling outside the area every day to work.

Years ago there were fourteen public houses in the area, most of which have been sold and made into private houses.

There are many very old houses in the area, the oldest one having been built in the 15th century and which is called The Old House. It was occupied for many years by Sarah Siddon, the famous actress. It was afterwards occupied by various families, then remained empty for many years and was in need of much attention. It was purchased in the 1970s by Mr Malcolm Collins from Cheltenham, who is still working to restore it to its former state.

Another interesting house overlooks the village, and is called Bet Kebir, which means 'Big House' in Arabic. This name was given to it by the late owner Mr George Jones, who worked for the Egyptian government. Most of his life was spent abroad, but on one occasion when at home, he insisted that he saw a ghost descending the staircase in riding habit. This was the talk of the village for many weeks, and has since been referred to as the 'Ghost House', even to the present day.

Lydbrook attracts many visitors with its lovely walks and scenery, and no doubt this is why they come back to visit so frequently.

Maisemore ❧

Question: Where can you stand on a bridge and watch half, only half, of the famous Severn Bore go by? Answer: At Maisemore, first village upstream from Gloucester, for, a short distance from here, the river divides into two, and enclosing the pancake flat island of Alney, the two halves wander along their separate ways for a couple of miles before coming together again at Lower Parting just below Gloucester.

At this bridge, the Bore, having lost some of its awesome power after the impact at Lower Parting, surges up the Maisemore Reach, lifting the trailing willows as it passes and nowadays all manner of daredevil tricks are tried out at the time of the Spring Tides: wet suits, canoes and surf boards being in great evidence along the roadside beside the river.

Very few win this battle, however, and in times gone by there have been many tragedies. Here, for example in 1785 a ferry carrying eight people back to Sandhurst from Maisemore Feast, capsized and all were drowned.

When Maisemore Bridge was built in 1956 it replaced the old stone bridge which was by then almost 200 years old, and, while the single concrete arch took shape, the traffic between Gloucester and Ledbury continued to rumble over the old bridge beside the building activity. When, finally, the old bridge was dismantled and the new one officially opened, an interesting cul-de-sac appeared where the road had to be re-aligned, and this was joyfully pounced upon by the 'travelling people' as a resting place for their caravans.

For several years, a running battle ensued between the caravan people and the local council, who first planted bushes on the strip of land (they were uprooted) then dumped boulders along the verge (removed) and finally dug a deep trench along the edge to prevent vehicular access and this, for the moment at least, has left the bushes to grow in peace.

This trench digging brings back echoes of a grazing dispute long ago between a 16th century Mayor of Gloucester and the Abbot of St Peter when a mob of townsfolk descended on the green pastures of Alney Island and dug a huge trench to prevent the Abbot's sheep from grazing there. It seems there's nothing new!

Maisemore, now, is an unbelievable hotch-potch of buildings of

103

many ages, thatched cottage stands beside modern split level, the beautiful old Ship House, once an inn stands intact, while other houses just as attractive have fallen into dilapidation and been replaced by new building. The old coal yard still operates beside the river, though now the coal is brought in by lorry instead of boat, and on the opposite side of the road five new houses bravely face the river, their shaved lawns going down to the river's edge.

At last, the Ministry of Works has begun to list some of Maisemore's surviving treasures, among them Court Farm which stands isolated from the main village, beside the church and village school (recently closed).

The church, although dating from the 15th century, and almost entirely rebuilt in the 19th, is now being re-roofed, so, like the village, it is going through continuous change, boasting a Norman font, a Jacobean pulpit, the royal arms of George III and now a 20th century roof!

On a small green knoll half way up the village stands what the passing motorist might be forgiven for believing to be a stranded upturned boat. Its pale blue lapped timbers cosily hugging the little hill top, it is, in actual fact, the Maisemore Village Hall, bought and erected in the 1950s with all the enthusiasm and optimism of these post-war years. Only recently and after much expenditure has it been brought up to modern standards of safety and fire prevention.

Milkwall 🌿

The village of Milkwall has had a long history of industry with its connections with steel iron ore workings, coal mining, lime quarry and burners. British Colour mining had a mineral crushing works. 1883 saw the opening of the Severn and Wye railway line where great use was made of it as a very busy freight line. It also had passenger trains from Coleford via Milkwall to Lydney. In the days before the Second World War practically everyone was related to one another in some way. They all worked at mines quarrying and at stone masons. Milkwall lies on the side of a hill and it was surrounded with oak and chestnut plantations; these have now been removed and mostly replanted with conifers.

After the war, more houses were built and the village was

changed by a large increase in population and new houses built. From the Mission Hall a new church was built. This has a fine stained glass window given in memory of the two brothers Powles who gave their lives. A Recreation Hall stands opposite which is used for many functions. The two village shops and butchers have been closed for many years but a very busy family post office is still here. The Working Men's Club was rebuilt, it had started out as a corrugated iron building. The Milkwall Football Club has been running for almost 50 years. They purchased their own ground and a prefab which they use for changing quarters. The old cooling pond from the steel works has been stocked with Dace Carp eels where the children have the right to fish without a licence. This pond has plenty of wild life – moorhens and during the season mallards and crested grebe call by and rest and feed. Small bats sweep down to drink, they are still in the steel works ruins and lime quarry. Badgers and foxes live along the railway line, rabbits and squirrels can also be seen. Jays, jackdaws, hawks, pigeons and owls, the occasional pheasant and plovers can be heard. Milkwall has, with the seasons, a change of beauty and colours and is still a friendly community.

Just on the edge of the village the Clearwell iron ore caves are of great interest and used for dances and barbecues; also Puzzle Woods which contain amongst the trees some of the oldest iron ore works known. These attractions are privately owned but open to visitors. The whole of the Wye Valley is within a few miles of the river Severn and like the old saying 'Lucky are those born twixt Severn and Wye, Too poor to live and too healthy to die'.

Minchinhampton 🎋

Minchinhampton has for centuries been a thriving community. Changes there have been, but the village with its medley of buildings from Cotswold stone cottages to grand houses, retains its old-world charm and sense of history.

Until the First World War there was also the manually-operated fire engine housed under the Market House. Firemen were summoned by the church bell and it was a case of 'first catch your horse . . .' grazing up on the common, before proceeding to quell the blaze. Today a telephone call brings the fire crew from Stroud or Nailsworth, achieving quicker though not such exciting results.

105

Mills manufacturing high quality woollen cloth brought wealth to the area and this probably accounts for the number of fine houses in and around the village. Longfords Mill still remains and amongst other cloths makes the yellow covering used for tennis balls. The mills and the houses owned by the gentry provided much of the local employment. Critchley Pin Mill at Brimscombe also employed outworkers in Minchinhampton to sort and card their hairpins and kirbygrips.

As in most small communities, the churches have played a dominant role in the life of the village. Part of the Parish Church of The Holy Trinity, with its unusual truncated spire, dates from the 14th century and was built on the site of a Norman church. Not far away in Chapel Lane was the workhouse. Needy families would go to Church Cottage to receive a ration of bread, distributed by the verger and his wife.

A new Baptist Church was built in the 1820s to replace the old Chapel. It was due to the efforts of its congregation and the then Minister, the Rev. S. J. Ford, that the Minchinhampton Institute opened its doors in 1907 to provide a place in which 'young people could meet for recreation and mental improvement'. Today there is a Youth Club and a Sports and Social Centre.

Long-time residents recall the Minchinhampton Band as well as itinerant entertainers – Zenith Comedy Company and Butler's Variety Show – who performed in the Market House and lodged with local families. The portrait of Sarah Siddons who once played here hangs above the stage in the Market House where the Minchinhampton Dramatic Society, celebrating its 60th birthday in 1986, continues to draw large and appreciative audiences.

In the late 1960s the traditional Minchinhampton Fayre was revived and this is held every two years. Main streets are closed, stalls erected, and Minchinhamptonians, old and new, don more-or-less medieval costume and set about entertaining the crowds in order to raise money for local charities.

Are there ghosts in Minchinhampton? Rumour has it that a phantom coach and horses drives up Well Hill though no recent sighting has been reported. But if Tom Long's spectre ever appears, it may perhaps settle the question as to whether he was a highwayman hanged at the crossroads for his misdeeds, or if it is the bones of a poor suicide weaver that are buried there. Meanwhile, his post stands high on the common pointing travellers on their way to neighbouring towns and villages in the valleys below.

106

Minsterworth 🌿

They say it's possible to ford the Severn at Minsterworth at very low tide and certainly at first glance, it looks harmless enough with golden sandbars and rippling shallows and Elmore Back not too far distant on the further shore. The reason for this optimism is the Church Rock, a long ridge of stone beneath the bed of the river at this point. In the days before this loop of the river was bypassed by the Gloucester and Sharpness Canal it was a difficult place for shipping, where, at low tide, they could only pass singly. In those days the river was a busy, though always treacherously dangerous place. A ferry plied constantly to and fro between Minsterworth and Elmore Back, which at one time formed part of Minsterworth parish, so closely were they connected. The village had both coal and stone wharves for you would be hard put to it to find stone for building on these luscious green banks.

Luscious they were, and still are, though often under water in winter. Amazing tales are told of times of high flood, as in 1947 when the whole village was evacuated and a herd of cows swam to safety guided by an R.S.P.C.A. officer and the farmer in a boat! Small wonder that a window in the church vestry portrays Jesus walking upon the water!

The church has had a long history of battling with the elements for, though first dedicated (to St George) in 1135 it was constantly being flooded and was finally burnt down after being struck by lightning and was completely re-built in 1870 with a floor four feet higher than the original building. By now, poor old St George was out of favour and the new church was dedicated to St Peter – more appropriate, one would suppose, to a fishing and farming community. In fact, the Severn salmon are delightfully portrayed, gracefully netted, on one of the capitals inside the church, perhaps a reminder that in Elizabethan times the parson was entitled to a tithe of the fish caught in the Severn.

Maybe the regular inundations have something to do with the rich fertility of the land. The pastures have always been prime grazing for dairy herds right back to when they belonged to the Abbey (or Minster) of Gloucester, and the Blaisdon plum and cider apple orchards are a sight to see. During the Second World War a voluntary agricultural camp was set up at nearby Ham Green for growing potatoes and the volunteers were rewarded with a visit from Queen Mary who, though not actually digging any potatoes herself, graciously consented to being photographed with them, thereby setting the royal seal of approval on their war effort!

Mitcheldean 🐾

Would you like to feel you are flying without your feet ever leaving the ground? You can if you take the road from Mitcheldean, which goes up the 'great wall' of the Forest of Dean, the vast panorama of the Vale of Severn growing and growing as you climb, until, at last, the road takes a sudden turn and you are looking straight into the heart of the Dean. Here, fold on fold of tree-covered ridges stretch away into the blue south-west while, before you, the road loops and twists away, disappearing into the greenery. At this bend at the top of the hill once stood the Point Inn with surely one of the most spectacular views of any pub anywhere. Now, it's gone, victim of the inevitable road widening scheme, and all that can be seen are the slabs of dark rock where the old red sandstone used to be quarried.

In a cleft at the foot of the 'great wall' lies Mitcheldean, its tall medieval church spire rising from the mist. The church, its oldest parts of Norman origin has been much loved and cherished through the ages and is richly decorated. A flood of brilliant coloured light from windows of different periods, a lovingly restored 15th century 'Doom' painting on the tympanum of the chancel arch, a splendid carved screen with angels, a huge modern reredos of grey green stone, and much, much more; all are witness to the continuous loving care this jewel of a church has enjoyed. But, although some of the little narrow roads that surrounded it still twist their way towards the hill, others have undergone a shocking change. Where, for instance is the dear old Lion House, once a coaching inn with a great arched entrance through which would echo the clattering horses hooves? In more recent years it was a youth hostel, a marvellous starting place from which to explore the forest. Now, a blank space, strongly fenced, the site awaits planning permission for a block of dwellings for the elderly, but at least the arch has been preserved to adorn the front of the new building. Opposite, the tiny Old Town Hall dated 1710 is still in vigorous use by many local people.

108

No one can talk of Mitcheldean in this day and age without mentioning Rank Xerox. This giant, sprawling at the lower end of the little town, once employed over 5,000 workers from all over the Dean. Now, with its workforce reduced to nearer 1,000, its fortunes still affect the lives of local people. Some of its huge buildings are now occupied by M.E.W.S. – Mitcheldean Enterprise Workshops – which, with an E.E.C. Grant has been set up to house local small businesses. Many are now gaining a foothold but it's hard going.

Above Mitcheldean, where the forest begins there is a paradise awaiting the geologist, and though the old iron mines have long gone out of production on Wigpool Common, their ancient shafts, a source of anxiety to the owners of sheep (and adventurous children) are rich with information for the student.

High up, at the top of Plump Hill, is the Wilderness Field Study Centre, once the handsome Georgian residence of the Colchester Wemyss family, now ringing to the sounds of hordes of children who are brought from other parts of the county to study pond and forest life, explore the mines, walk the way-marked forest trails set up by the Forestry Commission, and generally stir up the echoes and make their presence felt!

Moreton-in-Marsh

In the Domesday Book Moreton was mentioned as a hamlet belonging to Westminster Abbey.

The oldest surviving building is the Curfew Tower in the centre, dating back to the 16th century, which was used as a lock-up. It has an ancient clock and a bell which was rung at 6 a.m. and 8 p.m. every day. Sir Robert Fry, lost in the fog one evening, found his way to Moreton from the sound of the bell and left an endowment of £1 per year for winding the clock and ten shillings for ringing the bell. It was last rung thus in 1860 by William Webb who was town-crier, parish constable, beadle and sexton. He broke his leg whilst trying to lock up a drunk, which hastened his death. After 1860 the bell was rung to call the fire brigade.

Another 16th century building is Lilac Cottage in the area near the church still known as Old Town.

The Norman church was demolished, except for the tower, and rebuilt in Gothic style in 1859.

Both the White Hart and the Unicorn (now the Redesdale Arms Hotel) were coaching inns and in 1820 seventy coaches a week passed through Moreton, but by 1856 there were none due to the advent of the railway in 1848. The Stratford-on-Avon and Moreton Tramway was opened in 1826 and it is said that twenty thousand people were there when the first wagons arrived in Moreton.

The Black Bear is another old hostelry and is reputed to have a poltergeist.

At the southern end of the High Street stands the mis-named Manor House Hotel. It was never a manor house. Originally an inn called Bury's Inn, it was bought in 1628 by Francis Creswyke and became known as Creswyke House, and the family lived there until 1752. They had some illustrious descendants including our present Royal Family through Queen Elizabeth the Queen Mother.

In 1752 Creswyke House was bought by Benjamin Busby and, in this century, after being a dress shop for some years, it became the Manor House Hotel just before the war. Many famous people have stayed there but it has not been reported if they saw the ghost

110

of Dame Creswyke who is said to have haunted the building and grounds for two hundred years after she drowned in a pool.

Another ghost walks at the Cottage Hospital. This was built in 1873 and it is said that the first matron, who was most meticulous, still carries out her inspections.

In 1875 Dr Sands Cox bequeathed to the hospital the chair that Charles I sat in during his trial in Westminster Hall. In 1927 it was in danger of decay and was sold to the Victoria and Albert Museum for £550 and is still there.

John Sankey, born at Wellington House in 1866, was Moreton's most distinguished son. He was knighted in 1914 and from 1929 to 1935 he was the Lord Chancellor. When a peerage was conferred on him he took the title of Baron Sankey of Moreton-in-Marsh, and in 1932 he became a Viscount. In 1933 he opened the new post office and, in 1935, the offices of the North Cotswold R.D.C. He died in 1948 and was buried in the lower cemetery after a funeral service in London.

Naunton 🌿

Naunton is indeed a lovely village, strewn along the poetically named river Windrush. It has been said, with perhaps some justification, that if the river ran beside the village street rather than behind the houses, Naunton might be as well-known as its famous neighbours; but it remains much as it has done for centuries, a quiet, peaceful farming community largely untroubled by the annual tourist invasion of the Cotswolds.

With the Domesday Survey of 1086 came Naunton's first Norman lord, Roger Doyly, who erected a church on what is thought to be the Saxon site. The main body of the church was built during the 12th century and successive generations left their mark to give us St Andrew's as we know it today.

Naunton has a wealth of lovely old houses of the 16th, 17th and 18th centuries. Many, such as the Mill at the east end of the village and the rectory of 1694 at the west end, are known to be on the site of much earlier buildings. Overbrook, near the church, is believed to be the oldest house, while close to the Manor is Naunton's only ancient monument, the dovecote. Believed to date from the 15th century, the dovecote was built from rubble, with a stone roof, four gables and a small central turret which was apparently a lantern. The dovecote was restored about 1949 but is now sadly somewhat neglected.

Cromwell House has one tiny and slightly askew window through which Cromwell is reputed to have looked and thus given the house its name. The story may be legend, but it is certainly true that the house once belonged to the Aylworth family one member of which, Richard, was an active Parliamentary supporter. During the Civil War the Earl of Essex marched his troops through the village en route from Stow to Gloucester, and nearly two centuries later a Royal visit was recorded when King George IV passed along the top road in 1821. Present members of the Royal Family, particularly Prince Charles, have often hunted through the parish.

The Black Horse Inn of 1870 is a welcome sight to the many ramblers who come through Naunton and to the Morris Men who dance there at intervals from May onwards. An earlier hostelry, Naunton Inn, was for about a hundred years a coaching inn before becoming a farmhouse about 1910. Naunton also has its own cider press. Last used in 1939 just before the outbreak of the Second World War, the press is now part of a private garden but is still visible from the road.

Near the cider press is Parson's Bridge, so called because it was built by the Rev. John Hurd in 1820 to replace stepping-stones over the Windrush. Blacksmith's Bridge near the Black Horse speaks of bygone days. Less than a hundred years ago Naunton had two shops, two butchers, two carpenters, a shoemaker, a wheelwright and three bakers. Nowadays the post office stores caters for the needs of the village.

During the 19th century the Baptist Chapel was built, an unusually prominent building for a small village. In the same century one of the rectors of St Andrew's Church was Edward Litton, a friend of Lewis Carroll. Carroll is said to have frequently visited the Rectory and who knows, maybe some of *Alice in Wonderland* was written there. Near the Rectory, a house bears the name 'Littons'.

A stranger walking through Naunton could be forgiven for thinking that the chief pastime of the inhabitants is fossil collecting. The area is rich in fossils and many a garden and window sill boasts echinoids (sea urchins), ammonites or brachiopods. The recent finds at the nearby Huntsman's Quarries of the teeth of a

112

plesiosaur and the jawbone of a megalosaurus show that dinosaurs once walked this part of the Cotswolds. The quarries provided tile stones for Oxford college roofs in the last century and are still supplying building stone today.

Because of its situation and undoubted charm as an unspoilt Cotswold village, Naunton has been used on numerous occasions as a location both for films and television programmes.

Newent 🌺

Many of the beautiful timber-framed buildings date from Elizabethan times and the very attractive Market Hall was built at some time between 1649 and 1668, being on columns with a room above. It is believed that Cromwell quartered his troops here – presumably the men and horses below and the officers above in the room which is now used as the Council Chamber and is a beautiful example of the architecture of those times. In the 1900s the Hall was enclosed at the bottom and when the fire engine came into being the engine itself was kept in this enclosure but the horses were grazed in a nearby orchard where the Memorial Hall has now been built. When an alarm was sounded (generally by a distraught owner on horseback or even on foot) the horses had to be caught, harnessed to the fire engine and galloped to the scene of the fire, by which time the building would probably have been severely damaged. It is on record that on one occasion a horse dropped dead en route, which could not have augured well for the building then on fire! One hastens to add that nowadays Newent has a modern and very efficient fire service which is always on the spot in the least possible time.

The Church of St Mary the Virgin is another fascinating point of interest. In the porch is a portion of the shaft of a cross which is of the 9th century and inside the church is the 'Newent Stone' of the 11th century, which was discovered in 1912 during excavations for a new vestry. The details and trades on many of the tombstones give a fascinating insight into the occupations of the people of Newent in days gone by. In 1849 Newent had over 120 traders, who included a lady corset-maker, farmers, grocers, millers, joiners, carpenters, bakers, boot and shoe makers, blacksmiths, butchers, watch and clock makers, wheelwrights, nail makers, milliners, dressmakers, beer retailers, coal and timber merchants, iron-mongers, tailors, drapers, straw-hat makers, painters and plumbers. There was also a basket-maker, a bacon factor, a seedsman, a currier and a tanner.

The Tan House in Culver Street, dated 1697, was formerly the home of Edward Bower, who was master of the Tanners Guild of Gloucester. The presence of a canal office clerk, two wharfingers and a marine store dealer point to the significance to Newent of the Hereford and Gloucester Canal which had a short branch to Newent at this time. In due course this canal was replaced by the railway and much of its route near Newent taken over by the G.W.R. line from Gloucester to Ledbury. Royal Mail Coaches also ran from Gloucester to Ledbury from the George Hotel, which is the oldest public house in the town. Over the past 150 years many of these trades and occupations have disappeared but others more appropriate to modern living have grown up and Newent is still a thriving place.

Newland 🦋

Newland lies sweetly in its own secluded valley, its ancient church tower with five decorated pinnacles outlined against the green hillside. Almost unique among Dean Forest villages, it was not ravaged by the mining boom and mushroom building of the 19th century and, although Stowe Quarry makes a huge red gash in the hillside not far away, the little 'Cathedral of the Forest' and its graceful entourage of Stuart and Georgian houses have been left relatively undisturbed.

Newland – the origin of the name is obvious – began like many other forest villages as a new clearing in a valley in the far west of the Dean, and many stories are told of the thankless task of the Crown's representatives who supposedly collected grazing and pannage fees from the locals for the King. The foresters had many and devious ways of avoiding making these payments for they held that their sheep had every right to graze where they pleased, and their pigs (apart from eating vast quantities of acorns) were doing positive good by rooting about on the forest floor turning over the earth and encouraging new growth! In later years, the village

114

became the home of the rich, who, having made their money from industry and mining came to live here away from it all.

Their big, handsome dwellings, most of them in the rosy red or grey-green forest stone and draped in ivy, surrounded the hillside churchyard and trail away along the narrow roads towards Monmouth, Coleford or down towards Bream and thence to Lydney and the Severn.

Along the lower edge of the churchyard are the whitewashed 17th century almshouses founded by William Jones, a London haberdasher who willed that 'sixteen pious persons' should live here, being given money, clothing and lectures – for which last a huge imposing lecturer's house stands at the end of the row! Imagine those ancient foresters nodding in the sun while some earnest young preacher rolls out the obligatory sermon on which his livelihood depends! Neatly restored in 1954, the little houses are all now privately occupied.

Still here, though no longer a school, is the Old Bell's Grammar School, founded by Edward Bell in 1639 – though schoolmaster's names are recorded in the church from as far back as the early 15th century. The doors of Bell's Grammar School finally closed in 1968 and it has now been swallowed up by the Royal Forest of Dean School at Berry Hill.

A strangely incongruous note is struck by the sign outside the inn which looks down over the churchyard from across the narrow road. A huge and ugly bird displays its great bony legs and feathered rump outside the 'Ostrich', an inn which might have been expected to display the arms of Sir John Joyce whose 14th century table tomb is one of the many fascinating monuments inside the church, or even something Dickensian like 'The Coach and Horses'. However, perhaps 'The Ostrich' is appropriate, after all, to a village which had its head firmly in the sand while the Industrial Revolution whirled around the forest, devastating many another village as it passed.

Newnham on Severn ༄

Newnham was not always the quiet village on the west bank of the Severn that it is now; indeed it was once one of the five Great Boroughs of Gloucester. Since very early times a settlement seems to have existed on the site, and by Roman times it was a port of some importance, being used by them for trade up and down the river in coal, bark, wood and charcoal, brought down the Ancient Ways from the Forest of Dean.

Newnham reached its zenith in the early 19th century, when in 1807 a quay was built with a twenty foot wall as a mooring for the ships, many of which were built at Broadoak (just upstream from Newnham). Cranes and warehouses also sprang up to take advantage of the increasing trade promised by the fast growing railway system. The old tramway tunnel under Haie Hill was converted, and became the first railway tunnel in the world in 1809. Glass was made in the town, candles were manufactured for the Forest mines and Newnham throve on its river trade. Already in the previous century the rich merchants had built their elegant houses in what is now the High Street, and everyone was busy and prosperous.

As early as 1134 Newnham was considered a fit place for the coffin of Robert, Duke of Normandy, to rest overnight on its journey from Cardiff to Gloucester Abbey, and several kings have visited Newnham – William II, Henry I, Henry II, Edward II and Edward III. King John is said to have had a special fondness for Newnham, and to have presented the Great Sword, now in Gloucester Museum.

During the Civil War a Royalist Garrison was stationed in the church and in the Castle – the latter is no longer extant, but vestiges of the ramparts remain near the significantly named Castle House on the Green.

With the construction of the Sharpness Canal Newnham's trade was over. In 1928 the last barge, aptly named 'Finis', left the dock, which has now virtually disappeared, as has the old ferry point. Some salmon fishing still continues, but the canal and the shifting course of the Severn have almost eliminated river traffic. Now even the small Forest railways have gone, and though the main line trains still run behind the town the station has been demolished – an overnight disappearance we are told. No longer can the citizens of Cinderford come down to Newnham to enjoy themselves on the sands. No railway, no sands, no ferry.

The Victoria Hotel has a long history; parts of it date back to 1550 though the main building is 17th century. Now sadly stolen, there used to be a piece of stained glass on the staircase window

116

dating from 1660, depicting the fable of The Ant and The Grass-hopper; The Victoria also boasts the ghost of a chambermaid who hanged herself in one of the attics. At one time Newnham may have had as many as 20 inns, but most of them are now private houses and only three remain. Mrs Annie Wood, the authoress, often stayed in Newnham House, down by the river, and incidents from Newnham life occur in her famous play *East Lynne*, published in 1861.

Newnham has no great glories today, but its beauty and serenity, and the friendliness of its inhabitants, make it a spot that many would assert to be one of the pleasantest places to be found anywhere.

North Cerney 🌿

Visitors come from miles to visit the beautiful church of All Saints, North Cerney which overlooks the river Churn and the main Cirencester to Cheltenham Road. It stands as a magnificent tribute to our medieval craftsmen. On the outside walls of the church are two graffiti, probably late 16th century. One appears to represent a Manticore (a beast with the body and tail of a lion and the head and shoulders of a man).

Near the church stands what was probably the priest's house. It was three cottages but was converted to one house again in 1952.

On the opposite side of the main road stands the Bathurst Arms public house with a delightful garden on the banks of the river Churn. The village consists of one main street with cottages and barns built of Cotswold stone. Manor Farm, once the centre of village life, belongs to the Bathurst Estate as do the majority of the cottages, but these are gradually being sold privately.

Just below the C. of E. Primary School founded in 1844, stands the Village Green with a magnificent lime tree where in years gone by the Methodists held their annual 'Camp' meeting.

New houses have been built at the top of the village, near the Methodist Chapel, built in 1891 and still used for worship on Sunday evenings, and a number of council houses and bungalows.

The village which once had two builders yards, a blacksmith, wheelwright, undertaker, cobbler, baker and 2 shops now just has a post office with a shop and a police station. The majority of

117

people work either in Cirencester or Cheltenham, travelling by car or bus.

North Nibley

Its lucky inhabitants know that North Nibley is special among villages. Its setting is incomparable, its history distinguished and its people independent and spirited. North Nibley lies along a small plateau just beneath the southern edge of the Cotswolds. Below it, the whole of the Vale of Severn spreads its green acres with the Forest of Dean, the Malvern Hills and the Brecon Beacons rising beyond. The tall towers of the Severn Bridge mark the opening of the Bristol Channel, and on a clear day when they can be seen from North Nibley the view is balanced by the sight of the tower of Gloucester Cathedral in the opposite direction. Above the village, steep hanging beech woods give way to the smooth turf of the Wolds and here the Tyndale Monument stands guard.

The ancient farmhouse of Hunt's Court in North Nibley is claimed to have been the birthplace of William Tyndale, whose translation of the Bible into English cost him his life at the stake in 1436. The tall tower of Cotswold stone which commemorates his martyrdom was built on Nibley Knoll in 1866, and during the last two years the village has raised £20,000 to restore it completely. From the top of the tower on a fine day those who climb its 123 steps obtain a tremendous view. The monument, lying as it does on the Cotswold Way, attracts increasing numbers of walkers for whom it is a landmark on a magnificent trail through the woodlands and wide open grassy tops of the Cotswolds.

Nibley Knoll was mentioned in history before Domesday, as was the spring at nearby Bournstream which still provides fresh water for its fortunate owners. And Nibley Green was the site of the last private battle in England between warring barons: over two hundred men were killed when Lord Lisle and his troops were ambushed and overwhelmed by the Berkeleys. For many years, North Nibley was the home of Lord Berkeley's main land agent, the village being conveniently placed between Berkeley Castle and the manor of Wotton. When Katharine Lady Berkeley founded her famous Grammar school in Wotton it was funded by rents from land in North Nibley. The agent, John Smythe, rebuilt the manor which stands today as Nibley House and no doubt bright young-sters from his village were among those chosen to benefit from Lady Katharine's endowment. The strong contingent of Nibley children who travel daily to school in Wotton continue this tradition.

The Church of St Martin, built mainly in the 15th century lies at one end of the village with the original school, the chantry house, beside it, while on the other side of the village there is a Congrega-tional Chapel and plenty of ecumenical projects are shared be-tween them. Farming – rearing sheep and beef cattle, market gardening, orchards and forestry, provides employment for a significant number of the villagers. Listers Engineering Works at Dursley and Renishaws Electronics employ skilled craftsmen and more scientists from the local Atomic Power Station make their homes here. Artists and staff from the Wildfowl Trust at Slim-bridge live in North Nibley as well as a few retired folk and commuters who work in Bristol. This wide range of people gives the village a very special spirit: for any village venture support and help appear almost by magic because each person indepen-dently contributes what is needed. All in all, North Nibley is a Cotswold Gem!

Norton ᔕᕟ

The village of Norton lies in the Severn Vale, three miles from Gloucester and on the A38 road leading to Tewkesbury and the Midlands. It is a scattered village with roads shaped like a letter 'Y'; the stem is the road from Gloucester and then at Cold Elm the road branches out. One branch goes down past the village green with its trees and pond, this area known as Bishops Norton, and on via a very narrow winding lane to Wainlodes which is on the bank of the river Severn.

The other road is the A38 and from this there is a loop road which contains another part of the village; this is on a hill and is known as Priors Norton; the main church of St Mary's is built on top of the hill and from here there are panoramic views of the Cotswold Hills.

In the spring time, the elvers come swimming up the river on the high tides; these are like long silvery white thin worms and are considered a great delicacy. Thirty odd years ago, most of the elvers were sold locally; a man who lived near the river would bring round a bath full, resting on the frame of his bike and he charged about 6d (2½p) for a pint pot full. Now elvering is big business, and people in cars with elver nets on the roofs come almost in convoy to catch the fish which are sold to the elver stations, reputably for £7 or £8 per pound and then exported to the Continent and Japan.

In the 19th century a Methodist chapel was built on the green but when it became obsolete the vicar of Norton, who was here for over forty years, bought the chapel, refurbished it and gave it to the parish. It is now known as St John's.

When the Chapel was built, a Miss Webb who was living at Norton Court, was so shocked at a chapel on the green that she wanted another road built, so that she would not have to pass the offending building. It was this lady who gave the piece of land on which the vicarage was built. Her father was an M.P. and there is a memorial tablet to him in Gloucester Cathedral.

A path known as the coffin path leads from the green across the fields and eventually up a very steep field to the churchyard at St Mary's; it must have been very hard work indeed to carry a coffin up this path. There is a memorial stone in the churchyard to the men who died in the First World War and recently this has been renovated and relettered.

Many years ago, there was an elderly lady who kept the village shop. One night the shop caught fire and the lady had to be rescued. When the fire was put out her rescuers were reported to have found money hidden all over the place, even in the buckets which were hung up for sale.

Nympsfield ✣

'Nympsfield is a pretty place
Set upon a tump
And all the folk do live upon
Is ag pag dump.'

Nowadays Nympsfield is not a place of outstanding architectural beauty, and the villagers eat other things as well as sloe-and-suet pudding!

The village lies in a fold of the hills just off the edge of the escarpment, and Coaley Peak, the popular viewpoint with its magnificent panorama of the Severn plain and the Welsh mountains beyond, is within Nympsfield parish.

Nympsfield is roughly half-way between Dursley and Stroud, and at its highest point is 800 feet above sea level. It is a self-contained place, separated by three miles and a very steep hill from Uley, the nearest village. Although centuries ago it was a staging post on the route from Bath to Gloucester, it now lies away from main roads and heavy traffic.

Because of its relative isolation, Nympsfield is blessed with a strong sense of community. Many families have lived here for generations, and newcomers are absorbed into the life of the village.

The name, spelt 'Nimdesfelle' in the Domesday Book, has been interpreted variously to mean 'an open place on stony ground', 'the field of Nym', or 'a holy place'.

Nympsfield is a small village, of less than 400 inhabitants, and it has retained its basic shape for centuries. Front Street and Back Street meet at either end of the Glebe, a field which slopes steeply down towards the church of St Bartholomew with its 15th century tower.

Nearly every house is stone-built and many are very old, notably Bell Court, White Hart Court and the Rose and Crown. There are also a number of beautiful gardens in the village, but to the relief of the inhabitants, the village is not sufficiently pretty to be a tourist attraction.

Nympsfield is an ancient place and two Stone Age barrows give witness to this. A Roman road ran through the village and down the escarpment to the crossing of the Severn at Arlingham. Before the Norman Conquest there was a chantry at Nympsfield which was visited by pilgrims from all over the west country. John Smith, writing in 1639, says of Nympsfield: 'a manor neither great nor good, but worse and less without the old and rich chantry of Kinley wherewith it is now beautified'. There are records of the names of priests in Nympsfield since 1185.

Before the Industrial Revolution, many of the villagers were employed as broadweavers, and population reached its peak at that time. Other occupations noted in the church register include tallow chandler, cordwainer, blacksmith, baker, shopkeeper, pig-killer, maltster, carter and sawyer. Today's list would look rather different: dentist, teacher, social worker, shopkeeper, engineer, factory worker, newspaper editor.

Interestingly, women have played an important part in Nympsfield's history. During the Civil War, the squire, George Bridgman, who was a Royalist, fled to Cirencester to escape the Roundhead villagers, but was taken sick there and died. His widow lived on for thirty years or so, and seems to have made a benevolent impression on the people of Nympsfield, because for 200 years families continued to baptise their daughters 'Heaveningham' which was Mrs Bridgman's unusual Christian name.

In the early part of this century, two sisters, Blanche and Beatrice Leigh, made their mark in the village. Grand-daughters of the Catholic convert William Leigh, who bought the Ducie estate in 1844, the Leigh sisters built the Catholic church and school and brought the Marist sisters to the village. They were great benefactors and educators in Nympsfield, and they live on in the memory of many of the older people.

To the outsider, Nympsfield may seem to be a pleasant enough place, in no way remarkable, but to those who belong here it's a very good place to live.

Oakridge 🦚

Oakridge is comprised of several hamlets, Oakridge Lynch, Far Oakridge, Bournes Green, Water Lane, Iles Green and Tunley.

There is evidence that the Abbey of Cirencester had lands which were given away at the time of the Dissolution. Later several wills of former inhabitants indicate that they were clothiers and broadweavers or agriculturists in the 18th century.

The village is about 600 feet above sea level, somewhat isolated from other villages and nicknamed 'Little Russia' or 'Little Siberia'.

It was a village with no large landlord. The majority of the cottages have always been owner-occupied. Most are modernised, some are used as holiday homes. There are a few modern houses infilling empty plots, and traditional stone cottages with gardens surrounded by stone walls. Between the houses is a maze of footpaths leading around the village.

Many craftsmen, artists and poets have made their homes here.

Ernest Gimson set up a workshop for cabinet making and trained local carpenters and blacksmiths to his high standards. The famous artist Sir William Rothenstein converted a cottage and barn into a fine house, Iles Farm, using local masons, tilers and carpenters. The poet and dramatist, John Drinkwater, lived in Far Oakridge, and Max Beerbohm is well remembered taking country walks in city clothes including spats.

More recently Sir Brian Robertson and Sir Stafford Cripps made their homes here, and were familiar figures in the village, Sir Brian was Lord Robertson of Oakridge. Dame Margaret Weston, Curator of the Science Museum is a child of Oakridge. Her father was a headmaster at the village school which she attended.

It is still the home of craftsmen – jewellers, a weaver, a blacksmith, a bookbinder and leathermaker as well as builders and carpenters who live side by side with daily commuters to the towns.

The road to Oakridge ends at the village greens. There are two: Church Green and Village Green. It is a picturesque setting with lime trees growing there, the church on one side, the school opposite, cottages on another side and the house where William Simmonds, sculptor and puppeteer lived on the fourth side.

St Bartholomew's Church was built in 1837, one of several churches built due to the efforts of John Keeble. The Methodist Chapel was built at the opposite end of the village, in 1874 on the site of an older chapel. It houses the village Museum, where craft tools, photographs and relics of the past are kept, and also has a schoolroom which is used for smaller village activities.

There is a Village Hall, where dramatic productions, flower shows, whist drives, annual dinners and the like are held, and next to it is the 'Pleasure Ground' where cricket and football matches are held.

The Mill House is a reminder of the days when Oakridge had a silk mill to give employment to the villagers. There is nothing to be seen of that now. Beneath Oakridge is a network of caves, formerly stone mines, where men dug the stone for the walls around the gardens and the common.

Between Oakridge Lynch and Water Lane is a lonely house, Battlescombe Farm, known locally as The Pest House. This is a reminder of the time when it was proposed to bring smallpox sufferers here, and the locals taking the law into their own hands, prevented the ambulance from entering the village and set fire to the house. The police put a guard on the house and some men went to prison; but the hospital was established elsewhere.

The War Memorial is unusual as it is a water trough. Originally erected in memory of Mabel and Christopher Dearmer in 1915, the names of men who fell in two wars were added to it, in addition to the war memorial tablets in the church.

As well as the more famous there have been many well-remembered characters in the village. Many had the surname of Hunt or Gardiner. Some of these gave their names to the pathways near their homes, and such names as Maria's Pitch, Joseph's Hill, Rebecca's Hill, Sammels, Twissels and Back of Ollis are carved in stone and set in the walls. Another well-remembered character is John Peacey, a pillar of the Chapel, who learned to ride a motorbike at the age of 80. There are pictures of him leading Whitsun parades around the village with a small harmonium to accompany the hymn-singing. He was a shopkeeper, baker, and butcher.

Oakridge is a vigorous, energetic community with a strong sense of tradition. This is well shown in the parish magazine, *What's On* which reports the current events, as well as forthcoming attractions.

Oxenton

Oxenton is a small village which lies about 7 miles north of Cheltenham. It is conveniently situated to give a choice of shopping areas – Cheltenham, Tewkesbury, Evesham – and is only 4 miles from the M5 motorway which opens up routes to many other parts of the country.

The village is linked with Gotherington and Woolstone as a parish, the largest village being Gotherington.

There are 30 houses and 4 working farms in Oxenton with a population of approximately 100 people of all ages and occupations. There are no shops or pubs but there is a church and a small village hall which is used for meetings and for village parties. There is plenty of community spirit with the various fund raising activities such as open weekends, coffee mornings, etc., taking place from time to time.

In days gone by Oxenton must have been quite a thriving village. We know that the village hall was once the village school and we have recently been able to look through the school records which were very carefully kept and give quite an insight into early 20th century schooldays. There were also shops and a pub which have since been made into comfortable homes and a local blacksmith – the smithy building still stands today and is used as a garage-cum-store. The small church dates back to the 12th century and is surrounded by fields with Oxenton Hill directly behind it. It is said to be the only churchyard in the country to contain the grave of a murderer.

The village itself is a mixture of new and old buildings, some red-brick, some cotswold stone, interspersed with a few thatched cottages.

When Rose Cottage, Oxenton was recently renovated, love letters dating back to 1824 were found hidden in the chimney. These tell the story of a courtship between a young man from Cirencester and a young lady from Oxenton.

The letters are rather difficult to read and some parts are missing due to the activities of mice, but we learn that he walked from Cirencester to visit her and also sent gifts such as scissors, thimbles, ribbon for garters and a clasp for her waist. The last letters, dated 1826, tell of the birth of a baby boy, which must have been quite shameful in those days, and the death of the young man from a chest complaint. The letters themselves were originally folded and closed with a waxed seal. Some were also franked.

Painswick ✤

Painswick, known as the 'Queen of the Cotswolds' was recorded in the Domesday Book as the largest manor of the county, but it must have existed much earlier, as remains of a Roman villa have been found at Highfold (formerly Ifold) and prehistoric remains have been found by Painswick Beacon.

In 1086 the name was Wicke, also spelt Wyke, but later Pain Fitzjohn was Lord of the Manor, and as he did a great deal for it the name 'Payneswyke' was in memory of him.

The most interesting place to see in Painswick is our lovely church and our famous churchyard with its lovely yew trees.

Many of the tombstones are those of clothiers, because it was the cloth mills which made Painswick important for several centuries. There were 31 mills on the Painswick Stream and its tributaries and 27 of these were cloth mills. It was water-power 'a never-failing stream' that made Painswick important in the cloth trade, but when steam-power came into use Painswick suffered very much.

The church you can see, if walking in the churchyard, is a beautiful one. The tower has a peal of twelve bells and there is a tradition that if you are born within the sound of Painswick bells you are a Painswick 'Bow-Wow'.

Painswick has a Feast Sunday. The first one after September 19th, when Sunday School children join hands encircling the church and sing hymns as they walk round it. For many years it was a custom to have a 'puppy-dog' pie on that day, but what we usually had was a steak pie or a fruit pie with a little china dog on it. There are many stories about why this was done.

The Falcon Inn was recorded in 1816 as a place from which, for the benefit of clothiers, there would be 'Waggons Flying to London', and in this century coaches and later buses left from this point.

The ground where the War Memorial now stands was once known locally as 'Jumbles Den', and until 1840 was the site of the former Town Hall, a Blind House and the stocks. On the New Street side there were once four houses, including the Crown Inn, which were all demolished in 1881 to open a good view of the church.

Off New Street at the side of the church is Victoria Street, named in remembrance of Queen Victoria, but before that it was Pig Street, because where it entered George Court, pigs and sheep were marketed.

At the foot of Victoria Street stands Lovedays House, now the Vicarage and a perfect example of a small 18th century Cotswold family house, and Court House, another fine Cotswold building where the Constable lived and kept an eye on the stocks.

Going back along St Mary Street you come to the centre of the village known as the Cross with Tibbiwell Street on the right and part of the oldest route recorded from Gloucester to Bisley and Cirencester. Friday Street, once Bell Street, lies to the left. The Bell Inn and other old buildings were destroyed by bombs in 1941.

127

This area was a market place for years, continuing through the centuries into Bisley Street the most ancient road recorded. A fine medieval doorway is worth seeing.

Parkend 🌿

Parkend is a quiet village, lying in the lowest point of the Forest of Dean, midway between Coleford and Lydney – its population is about 700.

Its now peaceful appearance hides a fascinating industrial history, mainly of the 19th century, when the village had a thriving ironworks, tin-plate works, two stoneworks, a wood sawmill, and, within a radius of half a mile, a dozen coal mines. Through the village and around there was a complete system of tramroads – railway trains steamed in and out – and in those days Parkend was busy, noisy and dirty.

All the bustle and noise have now gone – but there are still many reminders of the past. The creeper-clad Dean Field Studies Centre owned by Avon County Council for school visits, was once the Engine House that supplied the blast for the iron furnaces at the iron works. This was acquired by the old Crown Office of Woods (now the Forestry Commission) and became the first Forester Training School in 1908, and until it closed in 1972 many hundreds of young men spent two years there undergoing training. Many of the students came from overseas, and in those days Parkend had quite an international flavour. Sadly, two Fijian students were killed in a car crash and are buried in Parkend churchyard.

Whitemead Park in the village, now a Leisure Park and Caravan and Camping Site for the Civil Service Motoring Association, has a history going back to the Middle Ages when it was over 300 acres with a hunting lodge. This was replaced in Queen Elizabeth I's reign, and in the 18th and 19th centuries it was considerably extended. From 1808–1969 it was the Headquarters of the Crown Office of Woods in the Dean, which then became the Forestry Commission, and throughout this period was the residence of the Deputy Surveyor who was responsible for the Forest. Lord Nelson was a visitor to the Dean in 1802 and the Duke of Wellington actually stayed at Whitemead Park in 1823. After 1969 the post of

128

Deputy Surveyor was combined with that of Conservator of Forests for the South West Conservancy at Bristol, and the offices moved from Whitemead Park to Coleford.

The only industries remaining in Parkend today are the Remploy Factory set up in 1949 for disabled people from all over the Forest. The old stoneworks site now has a flourishing caravan and haulage firm, and on the same premises where a wood sawmill has operated over many years, is now a depot where imported hardwood timber is kiln dried and stored.

The village boasts a thriving silver band and each year the whole village is involved in the annual Carnival and Fete on August Bank Holiday. The Dean Railway Preservation Society own the old railway line between Lydney and Parkend and when restoration has been completed it will run trips up and down, and this will provide a great tourist attraction.

Parkend is literally surrounded by forest. Walks abound and trees of many different species can be seen in the area where once forestry students learned their craft. There is an RSPB Bird Reserve at Nagshead just outside the village, and in the breeding season a resident warden lives on the site, recording and ringing all the migrant visitors. The area is well known to ornithologists and has one of the oldest nest box schemes in Europe. Here each spring come pied flycatchers, redstarts, and many species of warblers. Bird song has indeed taken over from the industrial noises of earlier years.

Poulton ✺

The village of Poulton lies midway between Cirencester and Fairford on the old coaching road between Bath, Bristol and London. It is a straggling village, stretching from Down Ampney to the south to Ready Token in the north; a place reputed to be the haunt of highwaymen.

The name Poulton means the 'Place on the Pool' although the pool no longer exists. By digging out the ditches and widening the stream, the houses at Ranbury no longer get flooded. In the old days, sewerage went into the ditches, and hence into the stream and the pool, causing many cases of diphtheria. Piped water only came in 1935 as did electricity, which was a very poor supply, each house being allowed three lights only and no appliances, until about 1967. Main sewerage came in 1969 but many houses are still on septic tanks.

Until the 1900s the village consisted of a few farms and their cottages, a Manor House, and the Priory, a mansion built on the site of an ancient priory. At the end of the 19th century, the church near the Priory was rebuilt in the village.

Before 1940 there was a school, two public houses – the New Inn (an Ale house) and The Falcon, fully licensed. In addition we had a post office with a manual telephone exchange, combined with a cycle shop and saddler; three grocery shops – one with a bakery attached; one with a butcher attached and one selling papers. There was also a separate baker. Previous to this time, there was also a blacksmith at the Old Forge, who made a gatepost about six feet high, composed of old horseshoes. Milk was brought around to the door in cans and measured into one's jug.

Now with many new houses and the amount of cars, we have only two shops and a post office and The Falcon. Most people now work in Swindon or Cirencester.

What was originally a tithe barn has been converted into a Village Hall, adjoining playing fields. There is also an excellent sports field known as 'Englands'.

The most interesting legend in Poulton is about Betty's Grave, which lies to the north of the village at the crossroads, and flowers are placed on her grave to this day.

Unfortunately two of our oldest cottages, on the London Road, were sold by the County Council and demolished. They had very steep roofs of stone, two rooms down and two up with exposed rafters. The road outside had been built up so many times that it was on the level of the window sills. In one of these cottages lived a quaint old character named Billy Weeks (who probably had never washed in his life!). He used to plough with a team of oxen. One evening he came to the door saying 'The Devil has a'come to Poulton, and he is hiding in my 'ood-pile. Will your husband get him out?' Of course it was only the shining eyes of a cat, but we managed to convince him the Devil had gone. He had a sister who lived at Honeycom Leas, about one and a half miles from the village, who walked to the shop every day to buy a loaf of bread, which she crumbled all the way home for the birds, and if she saw a snail or a worm in the road she would put it on the side so that it would not get run over.

130

Prestbury 🦋

Mention Prestbury to anyone and immediately Cheltenham Races come to mind for many people. The premier racecourse for National Hunt Steeplechase enthusiasts is at Prestbury Park, and is known worldwide for its feature races during the March Festival. Cheltenham races were originally held on Cleeve Hill, moving to its present site in 1831 when a steeplechase course was established in the park, at that time owned by Lord Ellenborough.

Many famous racing personalities have lived in the village including 'Black' Tom Oliver who rode three Grand National winners; Fred Archer, winner of many classic races on the flat; William Holman, Ben and John Roberts, Len Lefebve, 'Frenchie' Nicholson and Tim Hamey, all of whom trained racehorses. At one time over 100 horses were trained in the village, now, sad to say, no stables exist due to the urban development.

The Burgage, the oldest street in the village was part of the main road from Gloucester to Winchcombe when Winchcombe was the capital of Mercia. In 1249 it was granted the right to hold a three day fair in August, and in 1288 was styled a borough. A weekly market was also held. The street on the west side still has a row of thatched Yeomen's cottages. During the Civil War a Cavalier was riding from the battle of Worcester to Gloucester with tidings of the battle. Legend has it that he was shot in the chest by an arrow and killed. At dawn, on mornings in spring and autumn, the Cavalier's ghost still gallops through the lanes, and the sound of hooves is suddenly cut short near Prestbury House Hotel. This is only one of the many ghosts reputed to haunt the village.

Prestbury House, now an hotel, was the home of the Capel family who were at one time large land owners in the area since 1604. Major Christopher Capel, the last survivor of the family died in 1964 leaving the house and grounds for the benefit of retired clergy. A large complex of retirement homes has now been built within the grounds which also contains a local branch of the County Library. In 1925 Major Capel gave to the local Women's Institute the land upon which they erected a large hall which has been extended and modernised, and has become the main centre for village activities.

The Parish Church of St Mary dates back to 1280, although there was a church previous to this, mentioned in the Anglo-Saxon

Chronicle of the 9th century. This has been heavily restored on several occasions.

Prestbury has a sister church, St Nicolas, situated in Swindon Lane off the A435, opposite the entrance to the racecourse. This was established in 1930. A new church now stands on the site. Built in 1970 it is of octagonal shape, with a roof rising to a central apex. The present Church Hall has been added later, this serving the community very well as a meeting place for the Marle Hill Women's Institute, also for guides, brownies and senior citizens.

In the post-war era large areas of new housing have been responsible for the rise in population. These developments, being on the outskirts, have not detracted from the village atmosphere because a conservation order protects the more ancient streets.

Primrose Hill 🌿

Primrose Hill is situated on the borders of the Forest of Dean with magnificent views of the river Severn and Cotswolds. It could not really be called a village but a hamlet, being an estate built off the main Primrose Hill road from the town of Lydney. At one end of Primrose Hill is Soilwell House where Oliver Cromwell stayed. Unfortunately a famous barn was sadly burnt down several years ago but the foundations can still be seen. Opposite Soilwell House was a thriving brick works which is now a saw mill supplying pit props to coal mines.

Further down is Aliaston Court Farm which has a Roman road through the fields running as far as Lydney.

The Village School was built on land owned by Lord Bledisloe who sold it for £496. Church Services were first held in a pretty tin building. It was built largely as a result of the constant efforts and a long devoted ministry of the Rev. A. J. Lumbert who came to the area in 1893. He served the church for 52 years until his death in 1945.

Holy Trinity, the existing church, is a brick building which replaced the nearby tin building in 1933.

The thriving Women's Institute was formed in 1922. During the War one of the members was a Billeting Officer receiving children from Birmingham. Whist drives were held in members' houses to send comforts to Primrose Hill men serving in the Forces.

Quedgeley ✑

When Evelyn Cole was married in 1927 she came to live with her husband, John, in a small cottage in Elmore Lane, Quedgeley. John and his father were basket makers and thatchers and, in those days, their withy beds were close by, for this part of the Severn Vale, just three miles south of Gloucester, is low lying, flat and close to the river and canal.

There were three families engaged in basket making in Quedgeley at that time, for their products were needed in many trades – stout hampers in market gardens and in the fruit and vegetable market, great flat-bottomed baskets for bakers, grocers and the like, eel putcheons for the Severn fishermen and many, many more.

Quedgeley at that time was a roadside village – a few cottages strung out along the main road between Gloucester and Bristol and down the narrow lanes to left and right, a manor house, a couple of farms and a 13th century church a little to the west of the road.

Lush dairy country, this, with cattle being driven to Gloucester market along the main road on a Monday, 'one man in front to shut any gates that might be open' to prevent them straying from their path.

A peaceful rural life indeed, but, close as it is to the City of Gloucester, Quedgeley could not hope to survive unscathed for ever. In 1939 the RAF opened a maintenance unit on the east side of the main road, built houses for staff and became a major employer in the area. In October 1944 at the New Inn in Gloucester the 417 acre Quedgeley House estate with its Georgian residence, three farms and several pretty cottages was offered for sale by auction. Plans had already been agreed for house building on parts of the estate.

In 1962 a petrol depot with its pillbox storage tanks appeared beside the canal 'wrecking a beautiful field' says Richard Cole, still basket making in his little workshop beside the main road like his father and grandfather before him. Now the petrol depot is closed and being demolished. But Richard survives, his beautiful work in greater demand than ever and when a new pub was opened recently up the road it was named 'The Basket Maker' and he was an honoured guest at the opening celebrations.

Factories and installations of all kinds began to fill up the spaces along the road and canal between Quedgeley and Gloucester and then, in 1974 a veritable explosion of house building took place. Now, great wedges of those once smiling pastures have gone for ever. Streets and streets of tidy new houses fill the spaces between the old lanes, more and more building goes on and now, finally, a massive superstore beckons from the roundabout where once a few cottages stood.

This huge new community has grown so fast that it has not yet found an identity, though recent battles with the developers have brought a group of old and new residents together in a desperate effort to save one ancient survivor from the distant past.

Not far from the slender 13th century spire of the church, now standing curiously isolated among its ancient gravestones, are the remains of the moated Woolstrop Manor, also originally of the 13th century, one of the age old companions of the church. Not a sign of the ancient house remains inside the irregular shape of the moat but here, amid the faint whispers of far off times, in a tangle of trees and bushes and guarded by the deep surrounding water is a natural sanctuary for all manner of wild life. There is now a concerted campaign to prevent a developer from uprooting the trees, clearing the site, filling the moat and putting up thirty more houses.

Randwick ✒

A sunny day in early autumn and the leaves are slowly changing colour in Randwick woods. The first bronze and gold beech leaves are shivering on the hill-side above the village. In the Village Hall people are putting the last busy touches to the display for the annual Horticultural Show. Soon the judges will be assessing leeks, dahlias, cherry cakes and flower arrangements and later on Randwick people and their friends from round-about will be trooping round the tables to see who has won a prize-card, a cup, or the much coveted spade. It is the culmination of a lot of work for the village Social Committee and for keen members of the Gardening Club, but others have joined in too with their entries of knitting, painting, wine-making or photography, to support the event. Another successful Show is launched.

Winter months bring cold winds blowing across the playing field and the football teams practising on the sloping pitches. Randwick teams do well and have an enthusiastic following. In the church some of the young people learn to ring the bells, their sound rising through a dark winter's evening. The village church members have recently begun a 'shared-building' arrangement with the village chapel members, but have gone further than this in co-operation. Probably the main road up through the village will be icy and the bends in it treacherous if they are not gritted, but Randwick woods will be a picture-book scene for those who have time to look.

The spring flowers in Randwick woods are varied and beautiful and walkers on the Cotswold Way pause to look at anemones or violets. By the time the bluebells are in flower the village is ready for the big May events – the Cheese-rolling and the Wap Fair. Three cheeses are rolled anti-clockwise three times round the Parish Church, at a special service on the first May Sunday. This ancient, possibly pre-historic, custom was revived fourteen years ago. One of the cheeses is afterwards cut and slices enjoyed but the others are saved for the Wap. This fair held on the second Saturday in May, combines tradition, business enterprise, showmanship, craft, fierce competition and good-will. All the village turns out for this – stalls in the school play-ground, along the lane, and on the playing field.

In the summer's evening the Randwick Cub Scouts are tracking in the woods. Mysterious crossed sticks are to be seen, no doubt to be disturbed later that night by the badgers or foxes. Those relaxing in the Vine Tree garden look across the valley at the views of hill and common beyond. The wisps of smoke from bonfires drift upwards in the evening air, summer visitors have strolled through the village in the day, calling in at the village store (how lucky we are to have a first-class shop and Post Office!) and watching the children play on the swings. The steep pitches, winding between the houses and stone-walls, can make you breathless but the evening air is warm there. There are many 17th and 18th century weavers' cottages still standing, now renovated but keeping their air of bygone respectability and solidity. No clatter of looms now emerging from the open doors, though; the most apparent signs of village industry in the warm evening are those of the gardeners, still busy. Randwick today is probably a quieter place than in years gone by, in spite of summer traffic speeding through the village, but still a friendly place, a village with a community spirit.

Rodborough ✤

The area of the village is roughly triangular, bounded by the river Frome, the Nailsworth Stream and the third side going over the common on the hill between the two valleys. The old housing is based on the system of old roads which ran above the rivers on the spring lines with hollow roads (now footpaths) down to the valleys where the mills were. They are still the main source of employment.

The church dedicated to St Mary Magdelene is roughly at the junction of these two old roads, and apart from a perpendicular tower is 19th century, having been rebuilt after a fire. There are two non-conformist churches in the parish. Rodborough Tabernacle, which is now a United Reformed Church, was built in 1750 and altered in 1837. George Whitefield preached in the area and the Little Chapel opposite is said to have been the stable for the preacher's and elders' horses. The Scout Troop and Guide Company which meet here are amongst the oldest in Gloucestershire. In the hamlet of Butterrow there is a small Methodist Chapel built in 1856.

The original turnpike came up Rodborough Hill and joined the turnpike from Cainscross and went across the common, passing Rodborough Fort (a late 18th century folly) on the left. The road is now a track across the common. The old Pike House was a small cottage opposite the Prince Albert. It is now an outhouse for the house named 'The Pike House' which has 16th century origins.

The later turnpike from Stroud to London went up Butterrow Hill, the Pike House here was built in 1825 in the Gothic style and still has its last toll board with prices on it. At the top of the hill is The Bear Inn. The common is now owned by the National Trust and is used in the summer by commoners for grazing cattle. On the other side of the hill, below The Bear, is Rodborough Manor where lived Sir George Onesiphorus Paul, the Gloucestershire prison reformer who designed Northleach Prison, which is now a museum. Later, Lord John Russell, who was the Stroud M.P., bought the house in 1835. His son, Bertrand Russell, collected some of his parents' letters in *The Amberley Papers* and in one letter Lady Russell describes meeting a friend at Stroud Station in a dog-cart. One can still see why the friend insisted on walking as she was afraid the dog-cart would roll down the hill, as the road is a ledge at the bottom of the common. The Manor itself has been rebuilt after a fire.

Further down, in the valley, is the hamlet of Rooksmoor, which is a very attractive group of 17th century houses around Rooksmoor Mill. It was a flock mill and is now a furniture store etc. Going up the old road back to the church we pass the secluded hamlet of Kingscourt with its pub, The King's Head, then housing of the 1960s, Gastrells which is a mainly Edwardian hamlet, then Stanfields, a group of 17th century houses opposite another pleasant modern estate, and Stringers Court, a 16th century house. Rodborough Court, a prominent castle-like house was built in 1885 and is now an accountants office.

The mills in the parish were mainly on the Nailsworth Stream and in the 19th century many became small engineering firms servicing the cloth industry.

On the river Frome, in the parish, is part of the mill where the 'scarlet' is produced for the Guardsmen and the Swiss Guard. It is very active at the moment, because of the popularity of snooker, as they also make billiard cloth.

Ruardean 🦢

The author, John Moore, created a stir at the 'Maltshorel' in Ruardean when he innocently asked 'Who killed the bears?' and any modern visitor to the village would do well to avoid the subject altogether for the memory of this ugly incident of Victorian days dies hard and Ruardean folk bitterly resent the injustice of the blame being laid at their door.

The truth is that four Frenchmen, touring the Forest of Dean with their two performing bears, were set upon on the road by a mob of men and boys with sticks and stones. The bears were killed and three of the Frenchmen took refuge in Ruardean where villagers took them in, tended their injuries and collected money to help them back home. (The fourth man had run off into the forest in great fear and appeared some weeks later in Cardiff.)

But the story, as stories will, rolled around the country like a snowball, gathering embellishments all the way, the gist of it all being that two innocent little black bears, with muzzles on, had been killed at Ruardean. Since then, many a wag has got himself a bloody nose for making joking reference to the shameful tale when Ruardean men were present.

A proud little place, this, way out on the western edge of the Dean, its tall buttressed church spire looking out towards the Welsh hills, its terraced churchyard falling away towards the Wye. On the tympanum under the arch of the Norman doorway, a furious St George attacks a weedy little dragon, while just inside the door two beautifully carved stone fish were recently restored to the church when they were found forming part of the hearth of a cottage bread-oven nearby.

In the Sanctuary, a Davey Safety lamp burns in perpetual memory of the Arthur and Edward Colliery which was closed in 1958. In days gone by there were many small coal mines in the area mostly owned by free foresters. Harold Meek, himself a retired Ruardean miner, says there is still one little 'slope' working on the Pludds, a steep hillside outside the village.

The church, much loved, has recently been partly re-roofed with help from the diocese and restoration work is going on in the belfry. A recent visitor made the splendid gift of scarlet carpet for the aisle and sanctuary, but not all visitors are so generous. Some time ago, a lady cleaning in the church and searching for the choir's surplices which should have been hanging tidily in a cupboard, found them all in a heap under the altar, where it was obvious that they had been used as a bed by some passing tramp. Highly incensed, she went to report the find to the vicar, Patrick Birt who, in true Christian spirit replied 'Don't worry, Mrs H. the poor chap's got to sleep somewhere'. This kindly man has done a great deal for the church and the village and his parishioners were sad to see him leave for a larger parish in Wales.

Three pubs used to grace the main street of Ruardean. As Harold Meek puts it: 'The Bell to toll you in, the Shovel to cover you up, and the Angel to receive you into Heaven'. The Old Bell, however, is now closed and this pretty 18th century building opposite the church is now a hairdressing salon.

There are many roads to Ruardean, but the best is over Ruardean Hill, the highest point in the forest. Up, up and up you go through the mist, the trees now closing in on you, now falling away to left or right into deep bracken-filled ravines. Down the other side you twist and turn where little houses cling to the hillside, their gardens a veritable maze of paths, terraces and steps. Ruardean, they say, has grown up in a haphazard and untidy manner, but every little house shows the sturdy, independent character of the forester, who claimed his plot, and built his house and then defended it against all comers, and woe betide any 'foreigner' who hopes to buy one of these little old houses for it will take a very astute lawyer to untangle the complications of the deeds and bring the purchase to a successful conclusion.

Rudford ✿

The existence of a community at Rudford prior to 1066 is proved by the following entry in the Domesday Book:

'In the Botloe Hundred. Madog holds Rudford from the King. He held it himself before 1066. 2 hides. In Lordship 2 ploughs; 3 villagers and 4 smallholders with 3 ploughs. A mill which pays corn insofar as it can be sold. The value is and was 40s.'

In the latter part of the 18th century when the canal was being excavated through the Leadon valley a number of bodies were discovered but no explanation is given except that they were assumed to be those of men who had fallen in some of the many skirmishes which took place in this neighbourhood during the Civil War.

In the spring of 1868, on land owned by the Price family at Barbers Bridge, Rudford, workmen removing a hillock for the purpose of filling in a pool at its base found 86 skeletons which were re-interred in one grave on the spot.

As a result of this find W. P. Price, M.P., of Tibberton Court wrote a paper which was read at a meeting of the Cotteswold Club on 5th April, 1871. A copy of this paper can be seen in the Gloucestershire Collection at the County Library and makes fascinating reading.

W. P. Price says he has no doubt in his mind that the skeletons are the remains of men of Lord Herbert's Welsh Army, basing his theory on stories he had heard told by one Hannah Taylor, daughter of the village blacksmith who died in 1869 aged 97. Before her own death in 1871 Hannah passed on her father's story that his grandfather had been eye witness to the fighting which took place at 'Barbarous Bridge'. Many times as a child she had walked across the fields to visit Hartpury with her father and on those walks he had told her that if the mounds to be seen there were ever disturbed the bones of Welshmen engaged in the siege of Gloucester and slain on the spot would be found.

W. P. Price's theory is that on 16th March 1643 a party of retreating Welshmen met men of Waller's force and in the skirmish those whose skeletons were found so many years later died, giving the brook, stained by their blood, its name – 'Red Brook'.

Other skeletons have been found in the churchyard and under the Chancel of St Mary's Church, Rudford, and as W. P. Price argues, it seems reasonable to suppose that these would be the remains of the dead of Sir William Waller's force, who being part of the victorious army, were accorded burial on consecrated ground.

140

The communal grave of those Welshmen who came up to besiege Gloucester for the King and met their death in the retreat from Highnam on 24th March 1643 is marked by an obelisk built from stone taken from the ancient walls of Gloucester and stands high on the bank by the side of the road to Newent, at Barbers Bridge, Rudford.

St Briavels 🌿

St Briavels was once the administrative centre of the Forest of Dean and gave its name to the Hundred, upon which the Forest was based. The Forest proper used to extend beyond the boundaries of the St Briavels Hundred; now much of the Hundred, including St Briavels itself, is outside the Forest proper.

The castle in the village was built during the reign of Henry I. It was erected by Sir Milo Fitzwalter, Earl of Hereford; whose youngest son was killed during its construction when a stone from the highest tower dropped and crushed him.

The area was famous for hunting, being visited by King John, King Henry II and others. St Briavels was once famous for its 'Quarrels' or arrow heads. It is said that Henry III used six thousand in the year 1223.

There is a vague tradition that King John was a prisoner within the castle as there is a couplet inscribed on the cell wall:

'St Briavels water and Whyrals wheat
Are the best bread and water King John ever eat.'

Also in the prison there are drawings of three windmills and a treasure chest. Although there are no windmills in the area, there are three wells in the village. This may imply the presence of buried treasure, rumoured to be silver coins from the period of the Civil War.

One form of execution administered in the castle was 'oubliette' which means to forget. The prisoner was thrown down a 24 ft shaft, the trap-door was closed and death was from starvation, if not from the fall itself.

A unique custom associated with the village is the throwing of bread and cheese. Although first mentioned by Rudder in 1779 it is

141

much older, a possible relic of pagan rites celebrating the triumph of spring over winter. There is a piece of land in the neighbourhood called the Hundalls which originally belonged to the Crown. This land was given to the people of St Briavels for grazing and pasture. For those too poor to own animals and thus benefit from this land a yearly 'scramble' of bread and cheese was provided by an annual tax on those who used the land. (The tax levied was one old penny.)

The festivity still takes place on Whit Sunday. For three centuries it took place inside the church but because of the mess caused it was eventually moved to the pound wall outside.

The village also has several ghosts. The ghost of a young girl Emmaline, haunts Cinderhill House. In the times of arranged marriages, Emmaline was promised to an older man despite her own love for another. On the day of her wedding, whilst saying the vows, she suddenly ran out of the church, down Cinderhill to the well. In she jumped and was drowned. The well is barred and locked. The George Inn also has a ghost who walks along an upstairs corridor, making the sound of footsteps but there are no known reports of a sighting.

Sevenhampton 🌿

Sevenhampton village sits prettily along the upper valley of the Colne. Originally the village was situated on the opposite hill and was then called Sennington, but for some unknown reason, probably the plague, the village was totally destroyed and the whole population moved to a new site. Some evidence of the earlier village can still be seen on the hillside.

The hamlet of Brockhampton is larger and more compact, but together with its near neighbour it forms the Parish of Sevenhampton. The village became divided when Lawrence, of Sevenhampton Manor sold Brockhampton Park to the Craven family, who also bought Charlton Abbotts and its many surrounding acres.

Sevenhampton Manor was built for the Lawrence family in 1550 and is still a private house, though the south end was destroyed by fire in the 1950s. Brockhampton Park was built about 1639 and enlarged around 1865. It was for many years the home of the Craven family connected with Craven Arms, Shropshire. The Park was later owned by Colonel Fairfax Rhodes, but sadly it has now been turned into flats. This was carefully done without alteration to the exterior or the grounds, so from the outside it retains its former beauty. Inside two reception halls and the main staircase still retain their elegant panelling.

Transport in the old days was by horse or 'shank's pony'. Sheep were walked long distances to market. Pigs and cattle were walked to Andoversford too. The vicar was incumbent of several parishes and he walked between churches. Children walked to school taking packed lunches with them. If you needed to see the doctor a 4 mile walk to Winchcombe awaited you.

Entertainment was homemade with whist drives and dances at the Rhodes Memorial Hall in Brockhampton built by Colonel Rhodes. Originally it was one small room, known as the Reading Room, where men only could call each day to read the daily newspapers. The Hall was later extended in memory of Colonel Rhodes' son, killed in action during the South African War.

The Deer Park, which was at one time part of Brockhampton Park property, was famous for its herd of White Deer when the Gardner family were in residence. When the cricket club used the top end for their cricket pitch, they often had to carry the young fawns off the pitch before play could begin.

The Annual Produce Show in September is the highlight of the year, bringing out the best of vegetables, flowers, cooking, needle-craft and painting. With outdoor fun and games in the field behind the Hall.

Although it is now a Conservation Area, Sevenhampton with Brockhampton is not a tourist attraction. The Park gardens and lake are visually attractive and the church has a well-kept garden leading up to its main door. The village is pleasant to live in without boasting any spectacular beauty. It is off the beaten track and visitors have to make an effort to find it.

Sharpness ℘

It seems to be the end of the world, in spite of the fine new road that leads down from the A38 to lose itself among the dock-side warehouses and wharves just a stones throw away from the Severn. A hundred years ago, things were different. Then, a new railway bridge was opened, its twenty iron spans creeping out across the river to join Sharpness to Lydney and the Forest of Dean beyond. Then, the way was open for forest people to cross the river to work in Sharpness Dock, to move down to live in the little terraced houses built by the dock company, and to start a new community around the entrance to the Gloucester and Sharpness Canal which had been opened fifty years before to cut off the dangerous loops of the Severn and carry ships directly to the port of Gloucester.

In those days, with docks, railway and canal entrance Sharpness was booming. New houses sprang up on the ridge above the dock area, the huge Severn Bridge and Railway Hotel appeared on the headland overlooking the bridge, offices and shops and the little red brick church of St Andrew's all quickly followed, and Sharpness no doubt would have continued to grow had it not been for the shocking events of 25th October 1960.

That foggy night, as the flood tide raced upstream, two oil barges were carried up from Sharpness dock and crashed into the railway bridge, bringing down upon themselves a pier and two spans. Five bargemen died as the boats caught fire and finally sank,

144

and Sharpness has still not recovered from the blow. The rest of the bridge was eventually demolished and, now, at low tide, small remnants can be seen as well as the desolate remains of one of the barges, still lying in the sand.

A little way upstream, where the river and the canal run closely, side by side lie the even older relics of river life. Drawn up, side by side along the river bank at Purton, grass grown, half buried in the silt, lie the hulks of a dozen or more Severn trows – those graceful sailing barges which once plied their trade up and down the river as far as Gloucester and beyond.

Here, at Purton, where two swing bridges cross the canal, is the bridge keeper's house with its pretty doric columns, an exact replica of all the bridge keeper's houses along the canal from here to Gloucester. The Berkeley Hunt Inn faces the canal, while a few hundred yards away the 18th century Berkeley Arms looks out over Frampton Sands where the river, after a narrowing at Sharpness, suddenly grows to almost 2 miles wide and where the spectacular Severn Bore first begins to gather itself together for its surge up river towards Gloucester. Beside the inn lie the watery meadows of the riverside where the Severn Wildfowl Trust have a reserve for the flocks of wild geese and swans which come in winter to feed here.

But Sharpness is not content to live in the past. New plans are afoot (witness the excellent new approach road) to rejuvenate the docks. Coal, timber and cement are still brought in to continue their journey by road to many destinations. Many of the little houses, no longer needed for dock workers, are being renovated and let to the general public who may work elsewhere in the area. The 'Dockers Club' is thriving and a Marina has been opened. The canal is in constant use by smaller vessels and pleasure craft continuing the sixteen mile journey up to Gloucester, leaving the great sprawling loops of the Severn to their sandbanks, currents and calling waterfowl.

Sherborne

Sherborne was one of the Cotswold villages from which the religious houses in Gloucestershire derived their wealth, especially during the Cotswold woollen trade. In the case of Sherborne it was the Monks of Winchcombe Abbey who benefited. It is recorded that in 1485 as many as 2,900 sheep were sheared. The sheep were driven to Sherborne for the shearing season from the surrounding holdings as the villages were then called. Sherborne was chosen for this event as being the largest Manorial possession of the Abbey, and for the plentiful supply of water available in the river for washing the wool.

We can boast of having one famous inhabitant, James Bradley, born in the village in 1693, who later became the third Astronomer Royal. Noted for the discovery of the aberration of light mutation of the earth's axis, he also established the Greenwich time line, so presumably to him we owe the Greenwich Mean Time.

It was reported that a ghost used to walk the Monk's Passage in Sherborne House, and that John Dutton who was locally known as 'Crump' Dutton was to be seen driving a coach and horses towards Lodge Park House which was built as a Hunting and Coursing Lodge. Crump Dutton was reported to have been quite a gambler.

The present village stretches for just over a mile with almost all the cottages built on the north side of the street with the fronts facing south. It is actually split into two parts, commonly called Top and Bottom ends by the local inhabitants, with Sherborne House and the church in between. During the early 1800s almost the entire village including Sherborne House and the church adjoining it were rebuilt with much of the original local Cotswold stone being used. One cottage has a Norman doorway reputed to have come from an old Chapel which stood in the garden of one of the nearby farms. The village originally consisted of a large Manor House, 5 farms, 90 cottages, a mill with a bakehouse, four or five shops including a post office and a blacksmith's forge. As the majority of the cottages are now listed buildings, any alterations or additional building for modernisation purposes has been added to the rear of the cottages so that the facade has not been altered in any way, except the original small lattice windows have in most cases been replaced by larger plates of glass but the stone mullions still remain.

Sherborne House was occupied by the Military in 1940 and Lord and Lady Sherborne took up residence in the Manor Farmhouse in Windrush. After the war the House became a boys boarding school, followed by the International Academy of Continuous (Adult) Education, this was followed by the Beshara School of Intensive Esoteric Education and finally the House and adjoining stable flats have been sold to developers who are converting it into luxury accommodation mainly occupied by Americans.

In 1982 Charles, the 7th Lord Sherborne died leaving no heir; the title went to an elderly cousin who has since died, also leaving no heir so the title is now effectively extinct and the Estate has been bequeathed to the National Trust.

Shipton Oliffe
& Shipton Solers 🍃

The name Shipton probably derives from the Old English word 'scypen' which later developed into 'shippon' – a cattleshed or cowhouse. Oliffe and Solers are the names of ancient families. The Solers owned the manor as well as extensive lands in Gloucestershire back in the 14th century. The names Gyles, Robert and Ralph Oliff (or Olive) appear in the records in the late 17th and early 18th centuries associated with the manor of Shipton Oliffe. Both manors are listed in Domesday Book.

Close by each of the manors stands a church. St Mary's in Shipton Solers was designated the mother church. However, it later fell into disrepair and for fifty years, until 1930, it was used as a farm store. By this time, the Lord of the Manor and Patron of the two livings – long since united into one parish – was Mr Ernest Fieldhouse. He and his wife, Mamie, cherished the Shiptons for many a long year and the little church was fully restored in memory of his parents.

Shipton Oliffe's church, St Oswald's, went through bad times as well, although it never closed down. Many a summer fete was held close by in the manor grounds in the old days. Mr and Mrs Rishworth carried on this tradition in a number of ways and since they retired to Northleach they have been sadly missed.

Life in Shipton in the old days is remembered as tough but merry. There was the Brass Band; and a party of Mummers used to be formed at Christmas time. Then, at Whitsuntide, after a church service, the local branch of the Ancient Order of Foresters paraded in full regalia down to the Frogmill for a feast. Stalls with goodies, coconut-shies and other excitements were ranged at the roadside – all the fun of the fair for young and old.

Fred Stock used to make his coffins in a shed at the top of The Triangle. Mind you, if it was very frosty he made them in his own kitchen. To deliver a coffin to the church was a problem but they managed with a little wheeled trolley, preceded by Bill Cooper of School Lane carrying a lantern.

Shipton has long had a bus service. Rain, hail or snow, Jim Perrett's coaches have carried on regardless. Earlier on, his father-in-law used to drive a horse and van up and down to Cheltenham three times a week – a three to four hour trip. Jim's father, Walter, reported missing in the First World War, turned up eventually with a shattered foot and minus a leg. Once she got him back, his wife struggled in and out of town, taking the train at Andoversford, to shop for the family and keep the home going.

As soon as he was better, 'Peg-leg Perrett' carried on driving the horse and van until he'd saved up enough to buy a Model T Ford with a canvas top. As he was also sexton and grave-digger for St Oswald's, he too had a hand in Shipton's funeral culture. It seems they would yank one door off the Ford, thereby just being able to slide the coffins into the vehicle, converting it into a village hearse. Whereupon they would set off with dignity, followed by Bill Phillips in his own car for back-up.

In 1941, Jim Perrett took over and the business has developed from there into the considerable concern it is today.

Today, the baker, the blacksmith, the cobbler, the store and the school have all gone. But Shipton still has its Sports Field, and it still has the 'Reading Room'. Originally built for the recreation of the men and boys, it is now the social centre of the village.

Shurdington 🦢

When Elisha Philips used to cut the grass in Shurdington church-yard he always took care not to damage the primrose leaves among the long grass, thus ensuring a beautiful show again next year. Nowadays we do try, but our modern machines are quick

148

and ruthless and though they make a tidy job of the mowing, the churchyard flowers do suffer.

Spring comes early here, with first a carpet of snowdrops followed by the primroses surrounding the delicate needle-sharp spire of the old church of St Paul's which was founded before the Normans came and has been much loved and cared for throughout the ages between. It was much altered in the 14th century and, in 1896, when the spire was struck by lightning it had to be rebuilt. Even more recently the roof has been renewed and two enormous, ancient cedars in the churchyard have had to be destroyed, much to the distress of local people.

This was a world of orchards and farms clinging to the lower slopes of the western scarp of the Cotswolds, looking out over the Severn Vale towards Gloucester and the far Welsh hills. In autumn the air would be heavy with the smell of apples and pears, as every little farm and cottage had its cider press. One of the events of the year was Shurdington Cherry Feast when people came from far and near to buy the cherries and drink in the New Inn or the King's Head on the corner of Church Lane. The King's Head is gone, but the New Inn survives, much altered, and now renamed 'The Cheeseroller' in honour of one of the dafter local traditions when, on Whit Mondays, a Double Gloucester Cheese is rolled down the break-neck slope of nearby Cooper's Hill to be chased by anyone who dares!

The high ridge of the Cotswolds is always there, blocking the eastern sky and anyone who climbs up the old green road to Crippets is rewarded with a fabulous view out over the Severn Vale. Here at Crippets Farm, was the home of Edward Adrian Wilson of Scott's Antarctic Expedition and a stone was erected to his memory by his sister who also gave a guinea every year to the village school for the child who wrote the best essay about the expedition.

Further north along the ridge is the scar of Leckhampton Quarry, long closed, but displaying one of Gloucestershire's famous landmarks, the Devil's Chimney, a precarious looking pinnacle of rock, not, as one might believe, a wonderful natural phenomenon, but an extraordinary relic of the quarrying days.

Down on the lower slopes the village of Shurdington remained a small tight-knit community clustered around the church and strung out along the turnpike road from Bath to Cheltenham which was driven through village in 1820. Now, much of the farmland is considered 'ripe for development' and the population has leapt from a mere five hundred in 1939 to two or three thousand and still growing.

The little school beside the church was full to bursting and has had to be replaced. The village hall, built piecemeal from the ruins of an old malt house in Church Lane has also outlived its usefulness and a new social centre has been made in a building which housed agricultural workers and later Italian and German prisoners of war in the 1940s.

Old places have to prove their worth in the new scheme of things, or else they have to go, it seems. Pool Farm, with its placid duckpond and blossoming orchards, now, after a brief period as a Riding School, stands derelict whiles its new owners fight for planning permission to build on the land – yet, not far away, Little Shurdington Manor, owned by the Laurence family for generations is now the sumptuous Greenway Hotel with its moat and beautiful grounds and its own private helipad!

Siddington 🐚

The village of Siddington is small and one mile to the south of Cirencester. It has a pretty church called St Peter's dating around 1200 with many Norman features. The church was given to the Knights Hospitallers of Quenington in about 1200. Also by the church is an ancient stone tiled barn probably built by the Knights, soon after they received the property. The barn is thought (by some) to be the oldest standing in the country.

The church is situated on the eastern edge of the village near the Talkland school of Equitation, famous in the horse world.

On leaving the tree-lined avenue that leads from the church we pass Siddington Manor. The original house was moated but destroyed by fire, leaving no sign of a moat now. Village elders say a ghost in blue can be seen sometimes walking in the manor grounds.

Leaving the manor we enter the village proper and near a small antique shop we greet a grand house surrounded by a high wall and gate. This is Roberts House, once the home of John Roberts, one of the founders of the Quaker movement. Nearby stands a cottage and in its gardens lie the remains of a graveyard, the last resting place of John Roberts and a few other Quakers. The graveyard was first used in 1660 but is no longer in use.

We leave Roberts House and go past a row of red brick villas to enter the centre of the village. To the left is the shop and post office.

Opposite the shop is Park Way, a road leading past some modern houses and flats. Once a railway bridge spanned this road, now only the supports are visible. On past this and up a hill we reach the playing fields where many a game of football is played, and opposite this is another modern estate, once the site of the village pond.

On we go towards the outskirts of the village, once called Upper Siddington. Bordering the playing fields a road called the Butts leads to a tiny hump-back bridge which used to span the Thames and Severn canal (last used commercially in 1911). Now only ghost barges travel the canal as it has no water and much has been refilled. Over the bridge lies a farm and more stone buildings.

Past the Butts and on the right lies a little cottage next to a once busy farm where John Farmer the author once lived. Turning right past the cottage and along a narrow road bordered by trees and a field we reach the village C. of E. School. Walking past the school onto a gravelled pathway we reach the Old Rectory, near which St Mary's Church once stood.

Retracing our steps back to the shop and taking the road towards South Cerney, we pass more old stone cottages, once the site of the Blacksmith and Carpenters.

On the right, before the Village Hall, which was built in 1921 to commemorate the dead of the First World War, we pass another modern estate built on an old allotment site. Opposite this is another allotment where many men grow their vegetables and chat away on a Sunday morning. A track leads between the gardens to a few of the oldest cottages in the village.

Back on the road again we pass another modern estate on the right. On the left is a large house called Siddington Hall, once a private house with many servants, now turned into flats. Around the hall is a private estate called Frazers Folly, so named after the eccentric gent who built the hall. He added so many extensions to his home that it looked like a folly.

Beside the Hall is Plummers Farm. The house is a typical Cotswold stone dwelling, it has a stream bordering a pretty garden, where stands a giant Cedar of Lebanon.

Opposite the farm entrance used to be the canal, now filled in and built over. A short distance away is the Greyhound Pub another old building with a still intact mounting block on its outside wall.

This short journey through Siddington has hopefully whetted your appetite to come and explore for yourself.

Slimbridge ❧

Slimbridge is an ancient Manor of the Berkeley. Its old English name, Heslindruge, means track through the marsh. It has belonged to many famous people, either by dowry or inheritance. Its moated Manor House once stood on the site of the present day Rectory, behind the church. It was from that house that Maurice of Berkeley left to fight in the Battle of Bannockburn in 1314.

The church of St John, with its magnificent spire, was built around 1416, by the monks of Leonard Stanley. The fact that an earlier church had stood on this site is borne out by the discovery of stonework bearing Norman markings.

Inside the church, the Early English capitals are regarded as being among the most delicate known. The font is lead, 1644, and one of only nine in the county. In front of the west porch is an oaken screen, dedicated to the memory of William Tyndale, translator of the Bible, who, it is claimed, was born in the village at Hurst. Sadly this cannot be proved and it is most likely that he was born at Nibley, three or four miles away. Tyndale was martyred as a heretic in 1535. During his lifetime he made the promise 'that every ploughboy shall have the chance to read the Bible, as well as the Pope in Rome'.

Bishop John Stokesley, one of the main persecutors of the martyrs, and who personally saw to the burning of the translated Bibles, was Rector of Slimbridge from 1498, a time when Tyndale was a clergyman.

The parish of Slimbridge is made up of two villages and a hamlet: Slimbridge, Cambridge and Gossington. Cambridge was the most populated area in years gone by, as the village mill was situated at the junction of the Bristol to Gloucester road and the Dursley road, both being important turnpike roads, and the river Cam, a very advantageous position.

Cambridge has the only thatched cottage left in the parish, and apart from numerous old farmhouses, has an Elizabethan Manor called Rolls Court, which was built for a minor branch of the Berkeley family. It is probable that it was constructed with material from the medieval chapel of Cambridge, that was sold and demolished at the time of the Reformation. Lord Thomas Berkeley, whose effigy lies in Berkeley church, endowed seven chantries around the county, possibly in reparation for the murder of Edward II, and one of these was in the chapel of Cambridge.

There has always been an active sporting life in the parish, cricket and football clubs, tug-of-war, and a horse show, which has become quite an important event in the equestrian diary, and it is frequently patronised by members of the Royal family.

Thousands of visitors a year pass through Slimbridge to the Wild Fowl Trust, which is situated on the banks of the Severn. Peter Scott started the sanctuary in 1945 for the wildfowl frequenting the grasslands on the banks of the Severn. It is now a very important research centre, and many breeds of fowl which were in danger of becoming extinct have been saved. Set in a delightful park the birds can be observed at close quarters in natural surroundings.

South Cerney ༀ

Mentioned in the Domesday Book, 'Cernie' had 3 mills which are still here, but not in use as such.

At the beginning of the 12th century there was a small castle. The only reminders of it today are a boggy patch of land where the moat was, and two modern houses built on the site, called Castlegate and Moatside. There has been a church since the 9th century. The present building dates from the 12th century with 14th century additions. There is a stone Saxon coffin in the churchyard which was found during gravel extraction in the village.

In 1700 there were 120 houses with 500 people, 60 of whom were freeholders. In 1787 the Thames & Severn Canal came past the village, bringing coal and taking away butter and cheese. The barges were drawn by donkeys. The canal went out of use in 1927 but a lock house is still inhabited. Whilst in use at least 10 people were drowned. One, a child of two, was murdered by his mother.

The railway was built in 1883 and was of great use, until that too was discontinued in 1965.

In the last century the vicar moved from the vicarage in Church Lane to Liddell House. It was here that Lewis Carroll met Alice Liddell for whom he wrote *Alice's Adventures in Wonderland*.

South Cerney has its own mummers play which was handed down by word of mouth until 1913. It was revived about 7 years ago, but was found rather incomprehensible in places. 'That's how't be said.'

In 1862 six sheep-stealers were convicted in the village. They had been operating for many years; killing the sheep and hiding them in the box tombs in the churchyard until they could dispose of the meat and wool, and spreading ghost stories to keep people from the churchyard!

There are some unusual street names. The far end of the village is Upper Up, part of the main street is Clark's Hay and a lane by the river Churn is Bow-Wow.

Horse racing took place on Cerney Downs between 1781–1792. This area became an airfield, much used in the Second World War and today used by the Army.

During the last 50 years South Cerney has grown rapidly, mainly due to the gravel diggings. It is a friendly village with a well-mixed age range, from several 80–90 year old parishioners, retired and middle-aged folk, plus lots of young adults and small children. In all a very well-balanced community with lots of activity taking place.

Stanton 🌿

Stanton is fortunately tucked away up a little valley, withdrawn into the hills and you can go no further, unless you walk over the hills. Walkers on the Cotswold Way pass in their thousands but we are spared the noise, bustle and commercialisation of coaches and hordes of tourists. Less well-known than Campden, Broadway or

Burford, Stanton is one of a host of tiny, picturesque places tucked away in the hills.

Most of the ninety houses in the village were built between 1570 and 1650, the best period of Cotswold architecture, and they have been unaltered after restoration by Sir Philip Stott, who bought the estate in 1906. Nearly a quarter of the houses are used as holiday homes and of the permanent population of about 170, half are retired. They enjoy the amenities of a shop, pub, cricket club, horse riding, village hall, church and the Guildhouse craft sessions and concerts, all within walking distance in the coombe in the Cotswold escarpment. The number of farm hands and estate workers has declined in the last hundred years, and the country-wide exodus to the industrial towns has changed the character of the village population. The residents are very garden conscious, and open their gardens to the public on the last Sunday every June. The single street climbs gently to the crest of Shenberrow hill from which can be seen the Bredon and Malvern hills.

Stanton Court is a fine example of Jacobean architecture. The Manor House is a most beautiful building built in 1655. The site was part of the dowry of Catherine Parr. On two recent occasions a housekeeper saw a ghost in the Manor House. A small lady dressed in grey was in an armchair in the drawing room. On another occasion she was on the stairs.

Miss Eliza Wedgwood (1860–1947) was a notable resident of Stanton. She was the daughter of Rev. Robert Wedgwood, Rector of Dumbleton. He was grandson of the famous potter Josiah Wedgwood and cousin to Charles Darwin. Miss Wedgwood came to live at Stanton Court with her mother and sisters after her father's death in 1881. After her mother died, she moved into a smaller house then called Above Town, now known as Charity Farm. Eliza Wedgwood featured in Lady Cynthia Asquith's memoirs as a 'Cotswold Character'. She was well-known in the area, kind and eccentric. She concerned herself with the cottagers, and began a home-nursing service for them. The Tate Gallery has John Singer Sargent's painting of his sister seated at her own easel in the landscape of Stanton with her friend, Miss Wedgwood, seated beside her.

In 1906, when the village was becoming very neglected and dilapidated, the arrival of Philip Sidney Stott of Oldham made an enormous difference to the well-being of the inhabitants. He

bought the whole village and immediately began renovating and modernising the cottages. The village had gained a resident squire. Sir Philip had made his fortune from building cotton mills and other industrial buildings in Lancashire, Europe and Russia. He built a swimming pool for the village children, still in use today. He ran a coal and clothing club where people paid a few coppers each week into a fund and then once a year Sir Philip would have coal sent to Toddington Station from the coalfields, and then brought on to Stanton for distribution. Also rolls of woollen cloth for warm clothing were sent from the mills.

One of the most startling differences between Victorian England and the present day is the high mortality rate, particularly among infants. Tuberculosis carried off an alarming number of people. The villagers in the 1880s certainly were poor, but in a recently published *Blacksmith's Daughter*, Susan Oldacre writes that the poorest cottagers had a pig in the sty. Whereas most people now go outside the village to work, school and shop, in the old days the village was self sufficient, having its own dairy, bakehouse, lock up, post office and shops.

The Parish Church of St Michael & All Angels is an absolute

gem. Three pillars on the north side of the nave are Norman and much of historical interest has been added or rebuilt through the centuries. Sir Philip Stott's stewardship saw the complete refurbishment of the church by Sir Ninian Comper, the foremost ecclesiastical designer of the day.

Stanway 🌿

Nestling at the foot of Stanway Hill with its multi-greened blanket of Lidcomb Wood, Stanway village is a handful of stone cottages clustered around the environs of Stanway House and the adjoining St Peter's Church. Travellers along the Cotswold Way, which passes through the village, may be forgiven for thinking that it is a village left over from an earlier and more peaceful age and now quietly sleeping out its old age but it is, and always has been, a busy working village.

There has been a settlement on the spot for a very long time. 'Stan' is a Saxon word for stony and it is believed that a Saxon salt route, taking pack loads of salt from Droitwich to the south, passed through the village, so the name could be a comment on the state of the track. In the 8th century the land was deeded to the Abbey of Tewkesbury which set up an establishment there for four monks, a pleasant spot with running water which must have made a nice change in hot summers from the heat, smells and accompanying fevers which beset medieval towns.

In 1533 Richard Tracy of neighbouring Toddington obtained a lease of Stanway from Abbot Segar of Tewkesbury and between 1580 and 1640 the present house took shape. Despite problems during the Civil War the Tracy family continued ownership of the house until 1771 when Susan, last of the Stanway Tracys, married Lord Elcho, son of the Scottish Earl of Wemyss, with whose family ownership has since remained. Stanway is therefore notable in having changed hands only once, other than by inheritance, in nearly 1300 years. The present occupiers are Lord and Lady Neidpath, son of the present Earl of Wemyss.

There have been many alterations and additions to the property. A tithe barn was added in 1370 which still stands in very much its original form and today provides a useful hall for social gatherings, flower shows etc., rather than as a store for tithes. A

gatehouse was added around 1630 which was once thought to be the work of Inigo Jones but which is now ascribed to Timothy Strong of Barrington.

Recreation in the village has always been well catered for. The sporting can join the cricket club which has existed for many years or use the pre-war tennis court which has recently been renovated with money raised by voluntary efforts. The original cricket pavilion was an old railway carriage but J. M. Barrie of *Peter Pan* fame used to be a frequent visitor to Stanway and he was a keen cricketer and often played with the local team or brought a team of players to oppose them and showed his interest in a practical way by donating the present very pretty thatched pavilion perched above ground on staddle stones. One village player is reputed to have sneezed violently when leaving the ground after a match and then, to everyone's surprise, gone down on his knees and started to brush his hands over the grass. On being asked what he was up to he explained that the sneeze had blown out his glass eye.

St Peter's Church faces the front of Stanway House and during one of his visits J. M. Barrie had a bedroom looking out onto the church. Lying in bed one morning he was fascinated by a dancing golden image thrown onto his bedroom wall by the sun reflecting back from the golden cockerel atop the weather-vane and this, it is believed, was how Tinkerbell was born. The clock on the church nowadays shows a rather prettily faded blue face to passers-by which gives it a look of great age, but alas, the colour owes more to modern technology than age. Just after the Second World War the clock was repaired and while the face was at ground level one zealous parishioner decided to give it a good clean, using one of then then new-fangled biological washing powders. Unfortunately, old clock faces and new-fangled powders do not agree and the paintwork faded to its present colour.

As with most small villages, at one time people did not move very far but in recent years there have been some newcomers to the area who appear to have been successfully integrated. Perhaps the general attitude of Stanway residents to 'their' village can be summed up in the words of 'Gaffer' Edmunds, a retired game-keeper, who on being asked if he would like to join other pensioners on a coach outing replied 'I only left Stanway once, to fight for my King. I didn't like it much and since I got back I don't see any need to go away again. Thank you kindly but I'll stop at home'.

Staunton ❧

Whoever approaches Staunton Cross at speed does so at his peril whichever way he intends to turn. The motorist who comes roaring up from Gloucester towards the M50 must here make a blind turn to the left, almost touching the whitewashed wall of the old Swan Inn standing tall and solid right beside the road. If he wants to take either of the other roads, one meandering ahead through hilly country towards Malvern the other leading eventually to Tewkesbury, he must again brave that obscuring white wall and anything coming from behind it.

To make the situation even more hair-raising, two small shops face the Swan from across the narrow road, the only ones for miles around for the swelling population of Staunton and neighbouring Corse and there is always much coming and going, papers, posting letters, spending pocket money . . . , perhaps, some day, a little bypass will be made and the Swan and its carpark will find themselves in the middle of a roundabout or maybe the powers that be will decide to put up traffic lights, but, unlike the traffic, these matters move exceeding slow!

Between Staunton Cross and the church the road is lined with cottages and houses large and small of many different ages, some lovingly restored, one or two neglected, some modernised out of all recognition. But then we come to Ledbury Crescent. Obscured by trees and often passed unnoticed, here is a small piece of our more recent history. We here enter the hopefully ordered world of the O'Connor experiment of 1845.

Feargus O'Connor, a member of the Chartist movement campaigning for electoral reform went further than his fellows and planned a dream world where every family should have its own house and a plot of land from which to earn a living. He bought land in several local villages and divided it into equal sized plots each with a four-roomed bungalow and then persuaded some of the downtrodden industrial workers of those times to be his tenants.

Poor Feargus, his 'Garden of Eden' soon collapsed, beset with many problems, not least the discontent of his latter-day Adams and Eves who could not adapt to a life close to the land. The little houses have survived, however, and as grade 2 listed buildings have become part of our national heritage.

Near to the crescent is Staunton Court, beautiful in old age, its ancient stone steps decked about with flowers in summer but it is far from the sleepy relic of the past that it seems to be. Behind that lovely exterior beats the heart of a thriving wholesale business and the timber-framed buildings across the yard contain the massive coldstores where all kinds of dairy and poultry products are kept. A splendid medieval barn is home to tractors and trailers and a fleet of refrigerator vans, while brooding over the whole group is the church with its 14th century tower and spire. Some years ago, the tip of the spire was found to be crumbling and dangerous and the last few feet were taken down, to remain a tumbled heap of stones in the churchyard while the stump of the spire was neatly capped with concrete. Below the church looking out over a deep and wide pond is a huge and handsome timber-framed pigeon cote topped by a lantern roof through which the birds still come and go. It is said to contain 660 nesting places.

Stow-on-the-Wold

All the roads in Gloucestershire seem to lead to it, roads which in the days of Stow's great fairs would be thronged with horses, cows and sheep. The Market received its Royal Grant in 1107. Daniel Defoe tells of 20,000 sheep being sold here and 'there was no busier Market in all the Cotswolds'.

Sheep Street is one of the many alleyways along which drovers would herd their sheep to the 'sales'. By the late 15th century there were two annual fairs – always on a Thursday. The great horse sales have, over the years, drawn people to this idyllic setting from all over the world.

The stocks are still displayed on the green, rather the worse for wear, not only due to age, but also to the many visitors who love to sit in the stocks to have their photographs taken! One wonders if these self same stocks existed when the last great Battle of the First Civil War was fought in 1646. Here Sir Jacob Astley with 3,000 men marched towards Oxford, and here he was met and overwhelmed by the Cromwellians – who took him and 1,000 Royalists into Stow's church and imprisoned them there. 'Now' cried the old warrior to his captors, 'you have done your work and may go and play, unless you fall out amongst yourselves!'

In 1657 the church was declared ruinous and was restored in the 1680s and again in 1847 and then thoroughly restored in 1873. Some 12th century work still survives in St Edward's and the main features were established before the end of the 13th century.

Stow boasts a romantic pleasure garden of the 18th century with a wooded walk that goes through a tunnel and down to St Edward's Well. A ruined classical cottage lies in trees near a small artificial pond and stream. In the garden of Fosseway House is a folly with an embattled pinnacled tower like a small church. In Camp Gardens is a beehived shaped kiln and traces of an Iron Age hillfort. Gold and silver coins of Bodvic were found in the vicinity. Now coins of a different material can be found in the renowned sweet shop in the Market Place and in the beautiful new and small Talbot Court where home-made chocolates and sweets delight the eye and the palate of the customers. The fine old buildings in a variety of styles that grace this irregular square now house over forty antique shops. In Sheep Street is the Establishment of Lilian

Middleton, famous for her dolls' shop – her clients are worldwide. She also trains folk in the art of making dolls' bodies and heads in her Cotswold workshop.

'Stow on the Wold where the wind blows cold' is well named for it is the highest town in the Cotswolds – over 800 ft – but the end of the quote, 'and the cooks can't roast their dinner' is far from true. One has only to look at the number of tea rooms and hotels to realise that Stow is an example of true Cotswold life. One such tea room is St Edward's House, which has the most attractive facade in the Square. The wind may blow cold – but it's a healthy wind which brings prosperity to this lovely Cotswold village.

Stratton & Baunton

The village of Stratton with its small sister Baunton lie on the northern edge of the old market town of Cirencester, and straddle the old Roman road, Ermin Street, to Gloucester. Baunton has changed very little over the years, and is dependent for all its amenities on the growing village of Stratton.

The old village of Stratton was originally centred around the church which stands at the crossroads formed by the Gloucester Road and Baunton Lane which leads to the Cheltenham Road and the village of Baunton. Other development took place a little further south in Barn Way owing to availability of a good water supply. These two centres consisting of two groups of houses, many of them small wooden buildings, were called Upper Stratton and Lower Stratton and the field between was called Tweentowns.

In 1826 a new road to Cheltenham was built which commenced with a fork to the east of the Gloucester Road and half a mile south of Barnway. This road now formed a triangle with the Gloucester Road and Baunton Lane. Much building immediately took place around this junction, creating a new village centre with shops, a pub, a post office and a Village Hall.

In 1801 the population was 166, but by 1861 with so much more building it had risen to 468. Since the Second World War almost the whole of the triangle right up to Baunton Lane has been built on and the number of houses in the village at the present time is well over 1,000.

At the beginning of this century an important part of village life centred round the Malthouse where local beer was brewed. The building stood at the corner of Albion Street but was pulled down over 50 years ago. There was a bakehouse nearby where people could bring their weekend joints to be cooked. The village also had a wheelwright, an undertaker and carpenter employing five men, a blacksmith, a saddler, laundry, haulier, a coach proprietor, slater and a plasterer. In addition there was a corn and provender mill which is still in being today.

Meanwhile the church and school remained at the far northern end of the village somewhat isolated from the modern houses which had been built in the 1920s and 1930s and later in the 1950s and 1960s. Plans for a new school to be built in the triangle closer to the residential area were precipitated when the old school was badly damaged by fire.

Adjoining the newly-built school hall an attractive Village Hall was built as the old hall near the junction of the Gloucester and Cheltenham Roads had fallen into a bad state of repair. Thus the centre of the village has moved back towards the northern end once more, and with so many new houses and increased population both halls are in constant use by a variety of organisations and social events. The coming of a well-stocked general store and off-licence nearby, is an added amenity.

The church is mentioned in the Domesday Book but little of its Saxon origins remain. It was extensively repaired and enlarged in 1849, but in 1950 it was found the organ was nearing the end of its life. The Parochial Church Council were appalled when they heard what the cost of replacement would be, but happily a regular member of the congregation, Major Lethbridge Galton, decided he would make a gift of a new organ to be a memorial to his late wife. He was insistent that no other body be allowed to contribute towards it although it had been decided the organ should be built by the finest organ-builders possible. He then took the worried organist to the window of his house and pointed out a herd of cattle grazing peacefully in a field. 'They', he said, 'will pay for the new organ, I have sold them for £3,000.' It was then found the floor under the organ would have to be replaced to take the weight and this would cost in the region of £1,000. Major Lethbridge Galton insisted on paying this also, and after some weeks of negotiation a very fine organ was built and dedicated by the Bishop of Gloucester in October 1951.

Within the parish boundary was an old stone quarry on part of which gallows once stood. It was worked between the wars and the stone was found to abound in fossils. One of particular interest was the almost perfect specimen of a fish belonging to the Jurassic period and some 150 million years old. The quarry has now been built on but certain parts of it containing interesting stone formations and fossils have been preserved.

Taynton

Yes, a bustling life we had in Taynton then. Us old 'uns remember it well. See here the Potteries – bread crocks and bowls and garden ornaments we had there, and see the bricks stacked up. There's Mr Phillips loading his cart, ready for his hawking trip to Birmingham. Now, that path there, that's where all the courting couples come – Old Maid walk it's called. Can you hear Mr Smith shoeing those great farm horses? Come here – they've got one of these new-fangled steam engines at Hownhall – it pulls the ploughs backwards and forwards. There was a saw-pit there at Three Elms and a little shop in the front room.

This is the Church. My father remembers going to school there, and once it was struck by lightning. He said the stones were brought from the old church down by Taynton Court. Lots of tales he could tell. He said the old church was burnt down by the King's men in the Civil War, because the people here had stored gunpowder in there – what a thing to do. 'Twas more than twenty years before they had a new church. It must have been terrible. The Duke of Monmouth brought thousands of Welshmen here and hundreds were killed, they say.

My father told me stories too, of two men called Crockett and Horne, who held services in the Protestant fashion when Bloody Mary was ruling. Someone gave them away, and they were imprisoned, but Horne escaped, only to be caught again and burnt at the stake in Newent. I like the end of the tale – when Elizabeth came to the throne, the women of Taynton got the priest, tied him backwards on his horse and drove him, with sticks and yells and jeering, out of the parish.

They had spirit, those women of Taynton!

164

Tibberton 🪶

Nine hundred years ago the Domesday Book recorded that Tibberton (Tebriston) had a mill, plough teams, orchards and was owned by the Norman baron William Fitz Baderon.

Today agriculture is still the main industry though very few of the 600 present day inhabitants earn a living from the land. The mill closed in 1963 – one of the last village mills to survive into the second half of the 20th century. Tradesmen and craftsmen of yesteryear are, sadly, no more.

Today's inhabitants tend their neat lawns and gardens but not for a living. They are mainly commuters to the modern industries of Gloucester, five miles to the east.

In the last century it was horseback or the waggonette for a rare visit to Gloucester, perhaps to visit the market or fair. Then in 1885 the railway opened between Gloucester and Ledbury. Tibbertonians trudged across the meadows to their local shop at Barbers Bridge to ride the 'Daffodil Line' – so called because of its route through the daffodil fields between Newent and Dymock. A mock funeral party placed a wreath on the last passenger train to use the line in 1959.

Tibberton Court, a fine stone-faced mansion stands near the church. It was started in the early 18th century, then extended and altered several times until today it displays a classic facade and an Italianate tower.

It was the home of the squires of Tibberton, the Price family who supplied Mayors to Gloucester and MPs to Westminster for two centuries. They combined success in business and commerce with a rare concern for their villagers. They were Liberals and Unitarians, building cottages, almshouses and the village school long before the Education Act. One of the family, William Philip Price was an MP and the Chairman of the Midland Railway as well as a canal commissioner.

His grandson Morgan Phillips Price was perhaps the family's most colourful character. He refused to live as a squire at Tibberton Court, travelled extensively in Russia on behalf of the family timber business, and later joined in the Russian Revolution on the side of the Bolsheviks. On his return to England he became a

Labour MP, yet, strangely, he never lost his taste for fox hunting! He was also the recipient of an unusual gift – a live Russian bear!

New housing has saved Tibberton from the lingering death of many country villages. The village has a flourishing new school, Horticultural Society, and other organisations, but, strangely, no public house!

Tredington & Stoke Orchard

Low in the flat Severn Valley, facing the Malverns to the north-west, and enjoying wide, uninterrupted views of the Cotswold ridge to the south-east, Stoke-Orchard and Tredington seem to be the legacy of some Anglo-Saxon 'ribbon-development' along the lane that led from Bishop's Cleeve to the Ridgeway and old Gloucester to Tewkesbury Road.

Only one mile separates the villages, but as that mile was often muddy or flooded, and as Tredington traditionally gravitated towards Tewkesbury, and Stoke Orchard towards Bishop's Cleeve, there was a rift between them, geographically and socially.

Though so close together, Stoke Orchard and Tredington have each evolved a character as distinct as, say, the north and south of England. Stoke has a rich history, of which it is proud, but most of it is tucked away, up little lanes or at the back of its green, while it presents a vital, mercantile face to the world, thriving in the 1980s.

Tredington has an equal respect for mammon as its lush fields of Friesans, its acres of wheat, and its string of prosperous looking half-timbered old farmhouses testify, but it presents a sleepy, traditional face to the world, and affects a dignified disdain for commerce, except of course farming, and that preferably dairying, conducted in the most gentlemanly way.

Perhaps both villages would be very similar today had it not been for a chance development in the 1850s. Stoke's businesslike character probably owes more to luck than innate acumen, for in 1844 a railway station was built there. This offered secure jobs for the staid and opened up horizons and markets undreamed of for the adventurous. Even the smallest smallholder could take baskets of produce to sell at a good profit in Cheltenham. No doubt this bred a healthy respect for commerce and an inclination to let no opportunity be wasted. Buoyed up by its cider, which was legendary, Stoke embraced the industrial revolution with open arms and exuberantly allied its farming to shops and retail outlets anywhere.

Tredington, though only two miles away, was completely unaffected by this; the road was just too rough and muddy for easy travelling, so Tredington remained as isolated as ever, its neo-medieval way of life unchanged and Rice Duck (the village blacksmith) sole representative of industry until the arrival of a few motor cars in the 1920s.

The real meeting point of the village is Stagg's farm shop at Tredington where all the parish notices are displayed and all the vital news is passed on over the trays of eggs, lettuce and primulas, amongst a glorious harmony of babies, small children, mud and machinery repairs.

Stagg's farm was of course a favourite haunt of the one Tredington character who could out-deal the whole of Stoke without even trying. Inappropriately, it was Tredington, not Stoke that had the late and much missed Tom Pitman, whose steady rise from carter's boy to owner of 70-odd acres owed less to his industry on the land than his instinct for making a fast buck. He had spent most of his so-called working life as a shepherd, but not for him the quiet contemplative life. Never having heard of business studies, cash-flow, of creating a market, he homed in intuitively on anyone thinking of buying or selling anything, and always managed to profit from everybody involved, however remotely, in the transaction. Even in the 1930s, when the only four cars in the village were kept at the 'big houses', Tom was able to dazzle and impress everyone by appearing in a brand new Austin Seven Super Sports.

He aged with great distinction. Dressed always in a pullover with no front to it, a fawn milking coat, a copper bracelet against his rheumatism, and a wide-brimmed cowboy hat, he would cruise around all day in his Polski pick-up looking for anything promising. His success was so absolute that nobody in at least ten parishes had the slightest claim to social status or even acceptability unless they had been 'done' at least once by Tom. They were all there at his funeral. The little church was packed to overflowing and the service was taken by both a vicar and a canon (Tom never used to attend church, but both of them were 'clients'). Afterwards, they were boasting as loudly as the rest of the times when he had got the better of them. How Tom would have loved it!

Twigworth 🎣

When one of the travelling people was buried recently in Twig-worth churchyard his funeral procession caused a major traffic problem in Gloucester, as the whole company insisted on touring the city, calling in at all his favourite pubs before carrying him in splendour to this final resting place. Here, he was laid to rest as far away as possible from his old enemy, the patriarch of another travelling family, under a veritable mountain of floral tributes – set pieces which would have put the Jersey Flower Festival to shame. Although no headstone has yet been agreed with Twigworth Parish Council, the grave is permanently ablaze with colour even in winter when artificial flowers and leaves come into their own.

The graves of other travelling people in this churchyard can easily be recognised, with, here a splendid white angel, there a long inscription in immaculate gold lettering, crosses and wreaths and swags of flowers, always in the most expensive and beautiful stone. Smothered in flowers, real and plastic, they are a visible tribute to the clan spirit and loyalty of these travelling families, many of whom make their winter base here, at 'The Willows'.

Their colourful and exuberant life style is a source of constant anxiety to the P.C.C. who have to negotiate with the family fathers over the size and form of the headstone!

Who would have thought that the little grey Victorian Gothic church with its needle slim spire set among tall lime trees would ever have such exotic guests? It stands neatly beside the Tewkes-bury–Gloucester road, two or three miles from the city, backed by level fields. Beside it looms the huge stone vicarage, a veritable mansion whose fate is now in the balance since a cosy bungalow has been built in the grounds for the present vicar.

Close to the church, in the older part of the churchyard, is the simple headstone of Ivor Gurney, our tragic Severnside poet who lies peacefully here not far from his beloved river.

Although out of sight of the Severn, the land around Twigworth is so flat that the creeping floodwater has many times invaded the parish in the past. The little school was often surrounded and one old chap who used to drive a lorry along this road vows he has 'seen fowl houses floating about in the fields'. Nowadays the water

168

is hopefully under better control and Twigworth is a growing community owing, not least, to a huge, well-established and efficiently run mobile home park where many young couples have gladly made their first home.

Twyning 🦢

The parish of Twyning protrudes into Worcestershire, immediately north of Tewkesbury, the rivers Severn and Avon forming most of its boundary. The name Twyning means 'between two rivers'. The soil contains many fossils because this area was at the southernmost extent of the ice during the Ice Age. The countryside is very rural. From the parish can be seen the Malvern Hills, Bredon Hill and the start of the Cotswold range.

Although the church is in the oldest part of the village, it is not now in the centre. This moved to the area near the present village green after the plague and it is this area which has been developed most.

Twyning's growth during the 1960s was undoubtedly due to the construction of the M5 and M50 motorways, which meet in the north of the parish. Residents commute with ease to Birmingham, Ross-on-Wye, Worcester, Gloucester and Cheltenham.

Evesham and Bredon were more readily accessible in former times when a ferry across the Avon operated from the Fleet Inn. This was a pontoon-type construction which could take two cars and was wound across by a handle and chain. The landlord of the Fleet could be summoned by a gong on the far bank. There was also a paddle boat for ferrying pedestrians. It was not unknown for young men, returning from dances at Bredon in the early hours of a summer morning to draw lots amongst themselves who should strip off, swim the river and paddle the boat across, to save a six-mile detour through Tewkesbury. This ferry was out of action during the Second World War and though re-started subsequently was discontinued as people bought cars.

The church tower is of Norman construction and houses 6 bells cast by Rudhalls of Gloucester in 1723, the four heaviest being on a 14th century frame. The local ringers can earn themselves five shillings if they ring on November 5th. This was the date of the

169

death of the wife of the benefactor, Charles Hancock, who died c.1730. It has not been established whether this was to celebrate a happy union or the release from an unhappy one.

Twyning Village Hall is very close to the green, and was built originally by the owner of Twyning Park, which is a large house overlooking the river Avon, for her card parties.

The residents of the village are entertained during the week before Christmas by a group of carol singers, who cover as much of the village as possible, singing in unaccompanied four-part harmony. The money collected goes towards local charities and the church. The road to the Fleet Inn seems very long by the end of the week. Here it is that the carol singers gather finally, to enjoy the splendid hospitality of the host, rest their weary legs, thaw or dry out, sing the carols yet again and count the week's takings. This tradition started 30 years ago.

Local Estate Agents describe Twyning houses as being 'much sought after' and in a 'delightful river-side village'. It's not exactly Bourton-on-the-water, but it is very pleasant and we *can* call the village our own in the summer!

Uley ✣

This lovely little village lies at the farthest extremity of the Cam valley about two miles from Dursley. After Uley the road soars up to the top of Frocester Hill on its way to Stroud. At Uley the river Ewelme rises at the start of its short journey to join the Severn south of Frampton. It was the river which gave the village its enormous prosperity during the times of the great Cotswold Cloth trade. At one time there were over thirty mills between Uley and Cam and the population of Uley soared during the Napoleonic Wars when the people made red cloth for the army. Tradition has it that the valley also sold cloth to the French!

As the village is approached from the Dursley end you will notice a small outlying hill with a long stand of trees on top of it. This is Smallpox Hill and there was an isolation hospital built there during an epidemic at the beginning of this century. If you walk up there you will still find the ruins of the building at the top.

The greatest architectural treasure which Uley possesses must surely be Owlpen Manor, which is tucked away at the end of the

Owlpen Valley about a mile away from the main village. This beautiful medieval house is quite unspoilt. The house is famous for a very special legend.

In the year 1470 Margaret of Anjou, Henry VI's queen was marching north from Weymouth en route to the Battle of Tewkesbury, where she was to meet defeat at the hands of Edward IV who had imprisoned her husband in the Tower. The story has it that, she stayed at Owlpen for the night and slept in the room over the coat of arms which you can see from outside. The legend then passes to the present day, or at least to the time of the Second World War. It happens that the then owner of the manor had taken in evacuees to save them from the Blitz. It was her custom to kiss them goodnight and tuck them up in bed. One night she had to go to Uley and told the children that she would come up later to kiss them goodnight. Off she went not thinking much of anything that might happen.

Next morning the children came down full of excitement and shouted 'What a lovely dress you had on last night!' 'Tell me about it' said the lady. 'It was made of lovely red stuff' they replied, 'and you had on one of those tall pointy hats with a veil like ladies wore long ago.' It was then that she realised it must have been the shade of Queen Margaret. To those of us who know anything about the queen it hardly fits with the lady's warlike character, but who can say?

The manor is also supposed to be haunted by the Black Monk who, legend has it, was walled up and starved to death by the owners as he fled from the sack of Kingswood Abbey.

The manor is a private house and not open to the public but if you go round behind it you can enter its beautiful little church, a gem of the Pre-Raphaelite movement.

High above the village on the top of the scarp lie two splendid ancient sites. The first of these is the neolithic long-barrow known as 'Hetty Pegler's Tump'. This is a splendid example of its type with many chambers. Local tradition is that the barrow gets its name from a mad woman called Hetty Pegler who owned the barrow and sat on top of it hurling abuse at passers-by. Regrettably the contents of the excavated barrow were taken away and lost during an early archaeological dig during the last century. The other fine site is near the barrow at the top of the hill which leads down to Uley. It is a magnificent hill fort of the ancient British. It is a very large example of its kind and you can walk round its ramparts. Local tradition has it that it fell to the Romans.

Upton St Leonards 🐚

To people who are acquainted with this area very often their first thoughts turn to Bowden Hall, formerly known as Creed Place. One of the original owners was an eminent London Goldsmith, followed by Madame Rucker who built a school in the garden where the coachman's cottage stood. This lady provided fur tippets for the girls and leathern breeches and smock frocks for the boys. There followed a few more occupants, one being Lady Downe who was most generous in her gifts to the parish.

We have also Prinknash Abbey (originally called Prinknash Park), 700 feet above sea level, well sheltered and, in the words of Horace Walpole, 'commanding Elysium' with a private chapel. In the year 1850 the chapel was restored for Anglican worship by James Ackers who had bought the estate in 1847. Actually the chapel is of pre-Reformation origin; there is evidence that it was re-furnished for Anglican Worship in the 17th century. Mr Ackers' son sold Prinknash Park to a Mr Dyer Edwards who became a Roman Catholic in 1924 and realising that Prinknash Park was monastic property he offered the house and a little land immediately surrounding it to the Benedictines of Caldey Island. After many setbacks, and even the personal intervention of Pope Pius XI, in 1928 the Benedictines from Caldey Island settled themselves in. The bells which rang across the sea from Caldey now ring across the Upton fields. The house which had been recognised as a Priory was raised to the full status of a Benedictine Abbey in 1937.

In 1939 the foundation stone of the new church and monastery was laid by Cardinal Hinsley.

The first known resident clergyman was the Rev. Henry Parsons – 1833–1846. In 1889 much restoration was done to the church – the whole of the floors of the church were taken up, this was then concreted and then wood-block flooring under the seats, and stone pavement and slabs in the passages. Parts of the roof were repaired. A firm of bell founders undertook to put the fine peal of eight bells in good ringing order for £99.3.6. Six of the musical bells are from the famous Gloucester factory, each bears the date 1728.

As far back as the 18th century Upton had a school. Though its origin is lost, a tablet in the church refers to a Samual Smith, late schoolmaster in this parish: the date shown is 1794. Later in 1835 a Mr Parsons bought two cottages in the southern part of the churchyard, and converted them into a school. Shortly afterwards Lady Downe, who was living at Bowden Hall, bought the school cottage and in 1847 had plans drawn up for the school which is in use to-day. There were many village functions, apparently one of these was the Cherry Fair: stalls with cherries, gingerbread, etc. People came from neighbouring places and sports and wrestling matches were held, these causing disorderly scenes. Cherries were plentiful elsewhere along the road from Upton to Gloucester. In many features it resembled Barton Fair.

Those of us who live in Upton St Leonards to-day can count ourselves as being very lucky people. We live in lovely surroundings and know that there is so much history attached to the village.

Weston-sub-Edge 🦢

In the early 17th century Weston-sub-Edge was a small village having a church that was already 350 years old, a fine Norman manor house, a rectory, several stone cottages, and an inn with a coach house.

The surrounding Cotswold hills were covered with gorse and trees and each year the Cotswold Olympics were held on one, now called Dover's Hill, which attracted many thousands of people. This was a very important event having King James I as its royal patron, and it was with leave from him that Robert Dover had held his Olympics there, since 1612. King James is reputed to have given Robert Dover a suit of his own clothes to wear at the games where Prince Rupert was also a visitor. With some interruptions the Games have been held there since, and are now organised and run by the Robert Dover's Games Society in Chipping-Campden.

With these royal connections, the area was fiercely Royalist when the first Civil War began in 1642. Campden House, about three miles away was occupied by a Royalist garrison, who were concerned to maintain the link across the Cotswolds, between the

King's stronghold at Worcester, and his headquarters in Oxford. Parliamentary troops from Gloucester and elsewhere tried to break this link. The local villagers were robbed of their few possessions by both forces. They had taken the precaution of burying in the chancel of the church, the fine altar stone, being a single stone, eleven feet long and three feet wide, where it lay undisturbed for many years.

The Old Coach House was given to the village in 1930 for use as a Village Hall. During the Second World War it was used first as a billet for soldiers and then as a YMCA canteen. In 1981 it was decided to make use of the roof space to provide a games room.

The builder carrying out the alterations dug out a hole, two feet square, to take a steel girder to support the new floor. He dug up a piece of lead pipe, and thinking it was part of an old water pipe, threw it on the scrap heap. The next morning he picked it up again and looked at it and saw that it had been sealed at both ends, and when he shook it, it rattled. So he prised one end open, and out cascaded 307 silver coins and two gold, onto the floor.

The lead container had been specially made to hold the coins, being cleverly sealed down at the side and also the two ends. Inside was a scrap of parchment with the total £18 on, but unfortunately nothing else.

The coins were in excellent condition dating from 1547 to 1642 covering five reigns. The two gold ones were James I and the silver Charles I, Edward VI, Philip and Mary, Elizabeth I and James I.

An inquest was held and it was determined the find was Treasure Trove, as it had been buried exactly where the overhead beam and centre upright joined, so it was judged that the owner had buried them with the intention of recovery later.

They were valued at £5,926 and fortunately were purchased by the Cotswold District Council, with the aid of a grant from the Victoria and Albert Museum and they are now on permanent display in the Corinium Museum at Cirencester. The money went to the finder, the builder, but the lead case and scrap of parchment were deemed the property of the village, this was given to the museum to be included in the display.

Lots of speculations and theories were put forward as to the identity of the original owner, and what might have happened to him. Had he been forced to join the soldiers, or killed in one of the skirmishes? Records show that the garrison commander at

Chipping-Campden told the local populace that 'unless you bring me the monthly contribution for six months, you are to expect an unsanctified troop of horse among you, from whom, if you hide yourselves, they shall fire your house without mercy (and) hang up your bodies wherever they find them . . .'.

Perhaps these coins cost him his life. We shall never know and it's interesting to be left with a little mystery.

After a period of 340 years the events of the Civil War suddenly seemed to come very close to us, now living in this lovely peaceful little village.

Whiteshill &

Whiteshill is a village tucked away on a hillside overlooking Stroud in Cotswold country. The village is bounded by farmland and woodland and glorious views down adjoining valleys. It is a place of narrow streets, alleys and quaint cottages. Whiteshill is not a chocolate box picture kind of place, frozen in the past, but a thriving community which has developed steadily into virtually a suburb of Stroud in so much as the housing straggles down the hillside into Farmhill, Paganhill and Stroud itself in a number of styles.

At least until the middle of the present century the locals were a tight-knit community to whom village happenings were of far more importance than anything in the outside world. A number of older residents recall with amusement how there was often a gang of lads on the Plain waiting to throw stones or extract fines from those bold enough to pass the church coming up the hill from Stroud especially if it was a young man 'a courting' or the Police.

Today Whiteshill people work in a number of varied jobs mainly in Cheltenham, Gloucester and Stroud. In the past the local people would set out for work along footpaths still used today by ramblers. They were employed in stonework and quarrying towards Painswick, timberwork in Randwick Woods, farming and, of course, in the mills of Stroud. Whiteshill has always had its fair share of craftsmen and a regular Craft Fair held in the Institute carries on that tradition today.

At one time a number of shops existed. There was a bakehouse where the present post office is, a butchers and a Co-op (now the youth club). Next to the Woodcutters Arms Inn was a fish and chip shop where fish and chips were sold for 3d in 1935 and Mrs Asher's meat pattie for 1½d. Granny Cleaver sold faggots and peas and Star Green Cottage sold rice pudding by the slice. Two general shops and two pubs now remain.

Making their own fun was the order of the day. The locals tell endless stories of pranks played by youngsters. 'Tick tack toe' was a favourite one which consisted of a button on a length of cotton pinned to the putty at the top of the window. As the end of the cotton was pulled from the hiding place the resulting tap-tapping guaranteed an irate householder. The story of the Painswick people being referred to as 'Bow-wows' is said to be a result of a Whiteshill prank. The Whiteshill quarrymen, sick of having their lunches pinched by Painswick workers, baked pies which instead of the usual rabbit filling, were filled with dead puppies, hence the culinary delight called 'Bow-wow pie' which the Painswick men were supposed to have consumed.

The Whitsun Treat was an annual event for the children. The children would march round the village with the band, then down to Charlie Allen's (then MP for Stroud) at Farmhill where the children received three new pennies and a bun.

The Village Fete used to be held on the Vicarage lawn in summer and the Starton family, who built the Institute for the village, gave oranges and pennies to the children. Greasy Pole contests were also held, a young pig being the prize for the one who stayed on longest. Now greasy pole contests take place at the Woodcutters Arms on May Day and August Bank holiday.

The grandest village event nowadays is the street fair. The whole of Lower Street is closed to traffic and stalls are to be found along its whole length providing items for sale and entertainment.

Willersey 🦢

The village lies in a northern pocket of Gloucestershire between the wide vale of Evesham and the Cotswold Hills, near the start of the Cotswold Way. Its spacious greens, its ducks, its pond – all are known to travellers from far and wide but because there are few shops, few linger, except perhaps to feed the ducks or photograph the pond with its backdrop of mellow stone houses. The Aylesbury duck belong to the Parish Council, and when a fox makes a meal of one there is a whip-round to replace it!

Near the church is the post office with its mini-market, the hairdresser and the school, built in 1844 by the Earl of Harrowby and still going strong. The children daily walk down Church Street in crocodile to Pool House with its stone gate pillars beyond the pond and next door is Penderels which was given by Charles II to the Penderel family as a reward for favours received. Almost opposite is the Old Bakehouse, where in times gone by the baker allowed her customers to settle their accounts once a year after the 'gras' (asparagus) season was over, so poor were many of the villagers. One W.I. member vividly remembers taking her mother's cakes there to be baked on a Saturday and playing 'hide and seek' with the other children up and down Bug Alley (now no longer there) until the baking was ready.

On the site of the Old Smithy, a blacksmith's shop for 200 years, a seat was erected in 1935 to mark the Silver Jubilee of King George V. Its replacement in 1981, commemorating the marriage of the Prince of Wales was financed partly by public subscription and partly by the proceeds of a Medieval Fayre held in 1980. This was the second such event held in the village and both engendered a great deal of community spirit. Everyone dressed in medieval costume and were participants in the 'Pond Crossing Contest' in which ingenuity of craft and dryness of crew counted highly with the judges!

The willow or 'withy' trees still to be seen by our brook were grown for tying up the asparagus or 'gras', once cultivated widely here. Willersey Wake was held annually in June when the 'gras' season was over and the fair stretched from the New Inn down Main Street to Pike Cross. In 1901, just before the Wake began, someone died in a caravan on the green. This turned out to be the 28 year-old son of the Earl of Harewood, who had taken the name of Eric Leith and left his home and family to wander the country-side with the fairground folk. As was the custom, his van was burned in the rickyard and the horses turned out to grass.

Did the church bells toll for him as they did for humbler mortals? Three tolls for a man, two for a woman and one for a child. This single note sounded much too often 100 years ago judging by the stones in the graveyard. In the 13th century porch of St Peter's is a resting place for the coffin while the four pall-bearers were presented with black gloves by the sorrowing family. One villager records that her father had a drawer full of such gloves given to him over the years.

Quite a different note sounded out one day in the 1920s, when a local lady married an elderly black man whose seven sisters in their colourful African robes are still remembered to this day. Colourful costumes of a more theatrical kind were stored in the barn of a house belonging to Miss Nancy Hewins, who ran the Osiris Repertory Company, a troupe of actresses who toured from Lands End to John O'Groats in two or three white Rolls Royces and caravans for 30 years until 1964.

In the last 60 years the population has more than doubled and is now balanced more or less evenly between new and old residents. The village certainly deserves H. J. Massingham's description: 'Proper Cotswold, with its true old barn houses grouped around the green, like casual knots of worthies delivering gossip or weather lore through the slow process of the years.'

Windrush ✻

Most people have heard of the river Windrush, but not so many know that there is a village of the same name lying half way between Cheltenham and Oxford.

Today there are some 56 houses, though at one time there were considerably more, as two and sometimes three cottages were converted into one more suitably sized house.

St Peter's church dating from the 14th century has a famous beak-head archway and fronts onto a triangular village green. Six beautiful lime trees stand on the green and are some eighty years old. These were planted by the late Lady Sherborne and replaced a chestnut tree whose roots were damaged by stone cutters chopping their stones on them. At the turn of the century stone was still being cut from the local quarry but it was shortly afterwards closed down. The quarry entrance still exists in the woods near the A40 and indeed tunnels under the road. The village school also closed early this century and has now been converted to a village hall.

Very little work other than farming is available and most working people must travel to Cheltenham some 18 miles away.

One or two houses are reputed to be haunted, namely Pinchpool Farm and Ley Mary Farm, but by whom seems uncertain. Footsteps have been heard in certain rooms.

Windrush is a very closely-knit community and indeed when we celebrated the Wedding of the Prince of Wales with a barbecue the whole village turned out. Eight houses belong to weekend people, but they too look upon Windrush as home and join in everything. We are extremely lucky to live in such a peaceful, happy village.

Witcombe & Bentham

In 1275 Witcombe was chronicled as land belonging to St Oswald's Priory in Gloucester, and the old Roman Ermin Street is the boundary between Little Witcombe and Great Witcombe, now one village. This ancient drove road climbs Birdlip Hill where the village boundary is reached at the crest. As an important highway this road had many inns, convenient for the changing of horses, and a century ago present day Marlborough House was the Talbot Inn, with a sign which read:

'Before this hill you do go up
Stop and have a cheerful cup.
When down this hill, all dangers past
Then stop and have a cheerful glass.'

Since 1612 Witcombe Park estate has been connected with the Hicks family, mercers in the City of London. In 1790, through marriage, the family name became Hicks-Beach and descendants are today the owners and residents of the Park, taking an active interest in village affairs.

The parish church of St Mary-the-Virgin in Great Witcombe was built in the 12th century. The chancel and nave are Norman, with a north aisle added in the 15th century. The present tower, built in 1750, has six bells which are still rung today by a team of local ringers, some carrying on a family tradition.

It was the old custom on Maundy Thursday to beat the bounds of a parish. Such a perambulation took place in Witcombe on April 28th 1815. On June 21st 1950 a party of children from Witcombe School walked the same boundary, compiling a list of

179

present day names of fields in the parish, which differ considerably from those listed in the 19th century.

Little Witcombe and Bentham are bisected by the A417 road which winds up Crickley Hill to the boundary near the crest. In this area remains of the Iron Age are much in evidence, and a 'dig' on the hill is now revealing many interesting relics.

The church of St Peter in Bentham was built in 1869 in the Victorian-Gothic style and, at the foot of Crickley Hill, has an air of peaceful dignity.

Until the Second World War Witcombe and Bentham were compact communities but an influx of service personnel to the local Royal Air Force camp site and workers for the aircraft factory changed the structure of the villages. In the past local tradesmen had supplied village needs, but with bus services to Cheltenham, Gloucester and Cirencester local trade died out. Mr Charles Taylor, the last village blacksmith, closed his forge in 1916 and there is no longer a baker, butcher, or dressmaker.

The post office on Birdlip Hill was run by the Hearn family for over 60 years until closed in 1957, and is now housed in a modern shop built on a council estate in the village.

Some things do, however, still flourish. The Witcombe Cricket Club, started at the beginning of this century still has an enthusiastic team. The sport is played in a field off the Birdlip Road and the tranquil setting is an attraction for local residents.

It was here that the Witcombe and Bentham Flower Show was held until 1984, but now moved to the Village Hall and adjoining field. This truly rural occasion has been held for many years with classes in horticulture, arts and crafts, bowling-for-the-pig and other side shows.

Gymkhanas are held at Witcombe Park. In 1944 Mrs Smythe, mother of internationally famous horsewoman Pat Smythe, then living on Crickley Hill, organised a gymkhana at Witcombe Court in aid of Red Cross funds.

A link with the past was revived in 1972 when the Rector, together with parishioners, staged a pageant at Great Witcombe called 'Ermin Street Ghosts'. 'Roman soldiers' complete with a working ballista entertained visitors. Now a group of enthusiasts from Witcombe and Bentham travel around the country portraying in splendid detail how the countryside was defended in bygone days.

180

Today the Village Hall is the centre of community life, and residents, both young and old, are as active now as in the past.

Withington

The village of Withington is tucked into a deep fold of the hills and surrounded by beautiful countryside where sheep quietly graze.

Only the tractors break the silence of early morning. Later, there is the laughter of the school-children as they arrive at the old school-house built of mellow stone. Many years ago the building was used as the court house where minor cases of poaching, petty theft or land disputes were thrashed out and the offenders punished.

Behind the school-house stands the ancient Manor House with its perfectly matched gables. In the garden of the manor is a medieval dove-cote, the source of many meals of fresh meat for the family during the winter months. The old house looks down upon a perfect row of Cotswold cottages, the delight of visitors as they stroll along the lane leading to the church.

The church lies at the approach into Withington and opposite the manor. Proud and very old, it presents a striking appearance with its magnificent tower and surrounded by a belt of ancient yew trees. In the evening as darkness falls the floodlit church is bathed in a golden light and peace falls upon the village. Or does it? For Withington, like every respectable village, has its ghost. If you follow the road from the church down the hill towards the Mill Inn, famous for its hospitality, you come to the Mill stream and a house that used to serve as the old Mill for grinding corn. Here, there is a presence – a sound of heavy breathing that gradually gets louder and louder until after a while it fades slowly away. Only people of a nervous disposition seem upset by these events.

What or who can it be? It never strays but is always in the same place at the same time. Withington with all its charm and serenity nurtures a secret. Could it be part of the ancient nunnery that flourished many centuries ago near the church? Or perhaps a ghost from the large Roman villa that stood near Chedworth woods all those years ago?

So much history is wrapped up in the streams and stones of this lovely place.

Woodchester 🐛

Above the main road, half-way between Stroud and Nailsworth, lie the twin villages comprising the parish of Woodchester. Turn off the A46 at Station Road; though today you will look in vain for any signs of a station, for the once busy little line that shuttled goods and passengers between Stonehouse and Nailsworth, and later also Stroud, was closed in the mid 1960s. For nearly two decades weeds choked the narrow cuttings; then to the delight of the villagers the Manpower Services Commission sent a team of young men to clear the herbage and lay a cycle track where once the *Dudbridge Donkey*, as the local train was affectionately nicknamed, had puffed through the valley.

Above the cycle track the road rises steeply, past Churches' Mill, to the War Memorial and a sign pointing left to South Woodchester and right to North Woodchester. The narrow lane to the north was once the coach road, before the turnpike road in the valley bottom was opened in 1781. Once too, near here, ran a track from Cirencester to the palatial Roman villa in North Woodchester, passing the hollow where Southfield Mill House looks westward towards the Upper Mill with its millpond behind. Built in the 1580s and added to over the next two centuries, it is a pleasing three storey gabled house of Cotswold stone.

The Woollen Mill behind has disappeared but once was a flourishing business. In its heyday, Frederick, Prince of Wales, visited the house in 1750, and Sir George Onesiphorus Paul, the prison reformer, lived there for some years. The mill remained in this family nearly a century, for this was the zenith of the wool trade in the Stroud valleys. There were many mills following the stream along the valley, but as trade declined in favour of the large Yorkshire Mills other manufactories took their place, and now for example there is leather tanning at Frogmarsh, noteworthy for its wool-drying tower, walking sticks at Churches' Mill and Bentley Pianos at Woodchester Mill. The latter cloth mill was visited by George III in 1788, the King on horseback and Queen Charlotte and the three eldest princesses in open carriages. The King wore a blue coat with a scarlet collar, and a cocked hat with which he acknowledged the cheers of the people. But in raising his hand to do so, a large tear was visible under the arm of his Majesty's coat!

It was in 1793 that Samuel Lysons began excavating in the churchyard, having heard rumours of tesserae found by grave diggers. Detailed drawings published in 1797 revealed a magnificent villa, with two courtyards and sixty-five rooms, but the great pavement is the only area that has been uncovered since. It is nearly fifty feet square, depicting Orpheus and his lyre surrounded by circles of birds and beasts, all executed in elaborate detail. Pan is there too, and water nymphs, the whole enclosed by geometric patterns of great complexity.

The pavement was last uncovered in 1973, when over 140,000 people visited the site during the seven weeks it was open. It was a tremendous task for the villagers who provided car parking and refreshments, sold souvenirs and gave explanatory talks.

South Woodchester follows the springs round the hillside, an attractive grouping of 17th to 19th century cottages. At the southern end of the parish lies Woodchester Park, the later home of the Lords of the Manor, in a fold of wooded hills enclosing five lakes, well stocked with fish.

South Woodchester is a conservation area, and in the latter years there has been little new building there, the new estates being in the north, except for a group of old people's bungalows. Previously there had been a row of almshouses at the top of the steepest hill in Woodchester. No water was laid on during most of their existence, and the old people had to collect it in buckets from the spring at the bottom, an inconsideration that must have ensured a rapid turnover of inmates. Even the new bungalows are on a steep hill, with steps up to the houses.

This brief description reveals some of the attractions of Woodchester, whose visible history began with the Neolithic long barrow high above the village; Woodchester, whose name literally means The Fortress in the Woods.

Woodmancote

In the 1940s when Britain was at war with Germany we children carried our gas masks daily to school. Father had bought a suit, just as clothing coupons were issued. A lot of the men were going in the Forces. Woodmancote was quiet really, but the council houses were being built in Station Road, now privately owned.

One had to be very careful not to show light in the cottage windows, because of the war, but the good Lord still allowed the cowslips to grow in the meadow running down Station Road. Some men, like my father, were doing farming work. The land still had to be worked; up early at 5 a.m. Sunday was for worship, and we went each Sunday as a family — to Free Church (Countess of Huntingdon's connection). We grew to worship and serve the

Lord. When younger children were born, a neighbour would go with us. Friends helped support the less fortunate. One would find ways of earning 2/6d or so baby minding.

In times past, we would have a Sunday School outing to Stratford-on-Avon or Weston-super-Mare, and our grandparents would like a front seat in the coach. I remember having yellow and red cherries, it seemed amazing.

Today, Woodmancote has more people and houses, but the farms are just private houses, except for one or two. Manor Farm and Longwood are still working farms but Home Farm, Woodmancote Farm, Bottomley and Yew Tree are just homes now – but well preserved and cared for. It's good to see someone has the means to care for these and Bottomley Farm has been restored, making a lovely house. The Apple Tree is where couples and locals relax and unwind with a glass of whatever takes their fancy.

Woolaston ❧

In these days of round the clock radio and television programmes one might well wonder how villagers were entertained in days gone by.

The answer, of course, is that they entertained themselves and I am amazed at the amount and quality of entertainment that was available in Woolaston in the early part of this century.

Up to about 1920 the village school was the main scene for all kinds of functions. It was here that various travelling players, especially the 'Lauderdales' performed short plays such as *Maria Martin*.

It was in the school that the late Mrs H. Workman and her 'Gaieties' entertained villagers with their delightful variety concerts which were much appreciated. They had the advantage of performing on a portable stage, made for them by Mr G. Howell, the local carpenter, wheelwright, undertaker and general building merchant, and they took their concerts, stage and all to many villages in the area. Many of the older people in Woolaston will remember her troupe.

Children in the village went regularly to 'Magic Lantern' shows in the school and the Methodist Chapel. These of course, always had a good moral or educational slant, but they were none the less enjoyable for that.

Many concerts in the school from 1900–1910 are recorded in the Parish magazines – the varied programmes included songs, violin and piano solos, plays, ventriloquism etc.

There was obviously considerable musical talent in the village at the beginning of this century, for the rector, the Rev. Lambert wrote of one concert, 'This body of voices acquitted themselves very creditably, and, like the band, showed what they were capable of, with further training.'

Many concerts were given to raise money for an organ for Woolaston Church and once this was achieved frequent recitals on this new instrument were given by a Mr Whael, Mr Sully (organist at Chepstow Parish Church) and a Mr Maskell, making it possible for parishioners to hear works of the 'great master composers'.

In addition to these organised efforts in the village, many people entertained themselves in their own homes with cards and table games such as ludo, draughts, dominoes and snakes & ladders. Some cottagers owned pianos too, and the children learned to play.

There were some memorable characters in this village. One was Mrs Chivers who lived in a tiny one roomed dwelling at the foot of the steps of what is now Rock Cottage. It has now been incorporated with the main house, but 60 years ago it was a separate little dwelling, and mischievous children delighted in annoying poor Mrs Chivers by aiming stones and other missiles into her chimney.

Frequently across the Reddings stumbled old 'Erb Martin, who, today, would be classified as 'a vagrant of no fixed abode'. His 'home' was a cave in the woods above Barnage Farm. He may have done odd jobs for local farmers, but in those days, when there was no social security or unemployment benefit, he certainly 'lived off the land'.

In complete contrast to 'Erb was his brother Richard, 'Dickie' Martin, a founder and staunch supporter of the Methodist Chapel, where he was a regular worshipper. Children who attended the Sunday evening services were intrigued by his frequent punctuation of the preacher's prayers with interpolations such as 'Aye Lord, do Lord, bless the little children', and 'The cunning old rogue', this latter no doubt to emphasise some reference to the devil.

186

Another figure to be seen almost daily crossing the Reddings by the lower path was Mrs 'Jenny' Vickery, who lived in an orchard holding adjoining the field. Slim and nimble, she was quick-witted as well as sure-footed, and in response to the request, 'Give us a rhyme, please, Mrs Vickery', she would, without pause for thought, reel off a verse on some topical event, and then, executing a quick turn on twirling toes beneath her long, black, swirling skirt, she would go on her way. What a pity that her rhymes, which came so trippingly from her tongue, were not written down.

Mrs Vickery was famous also for her shrimps, which she carried in a basket on her arm to regular customers in Lydney and Newnham, often walking all the way. She even went as far afield as Berkeley and Sharpness, travelling from Lydney Town Station by train over the Severn Railway Bridge. She knew exactly how to cook shrimps so that it was no hardship to 'hud' them, and they slipped easily, plump and smooth and pink from their cases.

Another picturesque figure in the village was Mrs Vickery's husband, 'Bambry', who, with his wooden leg and lacking his wife's spritely mobility, travelled about in a donkey cart to ply his trade as a stone breaker. All day long he would be perched on a rectangular stack of stones, and the clanging of his hammer could be heard from afar as, with great precision, he broke the large stones into small pieces for road building and repairs. One of his regular work spots was on the roadside behind Pollard's (now Aveling Cottage) where the grass verge was wide enough to park his cart and leave his donkey to graze.

Wyck Rissington ❧

The parish of Wyck Rissington lies 2 miles south of Stow-on-the-Wold on the east bank of the river Dikler.

Delightful cottages dating from the 17th and 18th centuries are dotted along the edge of an expansive green, lined with horse chestnut trees.

From the early 18th century most of the village formed a part of the Wyck Hill Estate. This was sold and broken up in the depression of the 1930s and with its demise came the change of character to the cottages. These, previously lived in by farm labourers, waggoners, gamekeepers, and estate carpenters, were sold off for a minimal sum, and over the years were modernised. Cottages bought in the 1930s for £150–£200 now change hands – many to weekenders – for upwards of £100,000. Since 1939 only 6 houses have been built in the village. This being 'an area of outstanding beauty' planning permission is seldom granted.

The church, which is situated at the south end of the village, is dedicated, like many churches near the Fosse Way, to St Laurence who was martyred in Rome in AD 257. He was roasted alive on a grid iron, and a window commemorates this. A most interesting stained glass window in the chancel of the Crucifixion is early 14th century glass. The cross is of a rare green colour, and behind the figure are the sun, the moon and two stars. There is a theory that the sun is shown in eclipse and the moon is blood red. Mr Patrick Moore, the astronomer, established from old records at the Royal Observatory that there was a total eclipse of the sun in the year 1322, and it is thought that the designer may have been influenced by this.

The Reverend (later Canon) Harry S. Cheales was rector of the parish for 33 years from 1946. He was a learned and highly individual character, much respected. As the result of a vivid dream or vision he constructed a maze in the rectory garden in 1950. In this vision a very tall man stood behind his earthly agent indicating how the maze was to be made and its position in the garden. The plaques from the church were hung on the hedge at strategic points to guide the pilgrims.

In its construction Canon Cheales used 5,000 willow shoots to cover the 600 yards of path, and it was opened for the first time on Coronation Day. The maze represented the years of the pilgrim's life, progressing through childhood and adolescence, middle age and old age, death and Paradise, to Heaven. Before the Reformation the idea of the Path of Life was commonly represented by pavements inside churches and turf mazes outside, and a few of these have survived.

Each year on the Patron Saint's Day a procession was held around the maze, followed by a service in church and a performance of the children's rhyming games, one of which went as follows:

> The wind, the wind, the wind blows high,
> The rain comes scattering from the sky.

Jane is handsome, Jane is pretty,
She is the girl of Rissington city.
She goes a'courting one two three!
Please to tell me, who is he?

Kenny Smith says he loves her,
All the boys are mad about her!
Let the world say what they will,
Kenny Smith loves her still.

He takes her down the garden, sits her on his knee,
Says 'My ducky darling, what'll we have for tea?'
A china cup and saucer, a guinea golden ring,
A plate to put the porridge on, ding, dong, ding!

Sadly, when Canon Cheales retired in 1980 the rectory was sold off by the Church Commissioners and the new owners bulldozed the maze to make a private garden, but it is still mentioned in the guide books.

Index

191